This book is in remembrance of my mom,

Georgie Ann Walizer Forney

When It's All

Said

I0141647

and

Done

By Barbie Del Camp

When It's all Said and Done

ISBN 0991264215

ISBN 978-0-9912642-1-6

Contents

Introduction

When I first decided to write this book, it seemed like a good idea. Until, that is, the reality struck me…I needed to have something worthy of people's time. That's when the pressure began to sink in. Because I don't consider myself a "writer," I simply thought I would be one…as soon as I started writing! It was in this blissful state of innocence that the ball got rolling toward the completion of this book you now have before you.

It's one thing to pen thoughts on paper, with regard to my (our) story….it's another to think others will want to know about it. After all, EVERYONE has stories of trials and loss. "What's different about yours, and why should anyone care?" my inner voice kept saying to me.

It's a fair question…one that I ask myself to this day.

The simple answer might be in where hope was found, during what was easily the saddest, most profoundly tragic experience of my lifetime.

I needed to have a story that the reader will feel better off for having read. Simply put, I felt the need to share that hope.

Regardless of the affliction, whether cancer, Alzheimer's, or any other life threatening illness, the prolonged decline and eventual loss of a loved one leaves the closest survivors with an almost unimaginable sense of sadness and grief. This is my story, but there are so many others. No two are ever the same.

As you read this book, you'll notice a fair amount of "God-talk." Make no mistake, it is intentional, as both my husband Dave, and I are unapologetically, bible believing Christians. If anyone reading this is the least bit "put-off" by it, you're not alone. What you might find surprising is that you might be joined by others who call themselves "Christians"….yet disregard the humble submission to Jesus the Messiah, which is necessary. Still, out of those who do, there continue to be many who disregard the Bible as the only (and FINAL) authority where doctrine is concerned.

We often look back at where we came from and wonder at how long it took us to "finally get it right." Becoming Christians opened our world up like an oyster, but like many things, it is a constant process which involves growing, learning about and drawing closer to God. We've been through many challenges and periods of testing throughout, but have held onto our faith and trust in God's will throughout each trial. Each time, HE has sustained us. Salvation is a free gift that we accepted years ago. We now understand that it is the most important gift anyone can ever ask for, or accept.

Regardless of where the reader is regarding their faith, I hope you are able to glean some helpful information in these pages, on what you might expect to encounter…especially if you are experiencing similar circumstances with a loved one.

This compilation of thoughts on my experiences could not be possible without the patience and understanding of those who supported me throughout this process. My dear Father, who still struggles with picking up the pieces of his life without his wife, is first and foremost among them. Our shared experiences are interwoven throughout this body of work, and my hope is that his perspective is well represented. Like so many who have borne firsthand witness to this debilitating disease, his healing continues to be an ongoing process. My hope and prayer is that this will contribute to that end.

My husband Dave, was instrumental in editing this body of work. Like myself, he had no prior experience in anything close to this. The fact that he chose to dedicate himself to helping me organize and articulate my thoughts is yet another reason why I love him so much!

Martha Jackson, one of Mom's good friends, was a constant in her life during her last days. If ever there was someone who we could all have to visit, talk to, or smile with during challenging moments in our lives…that person would be a Martha Jackson. Her constant kindness was a source of joy; not only for my mother, but for the rest of our family as well.

The town of Bridgton, Maine, has been a Godsend for my father during the difficult days following the loss of my mother. Barely a day went by without someone greeting him with a hug, an attentive ear, or some words of genuine sympathy. I have a gained a new respect and appreciation for those folks in that small Maine community. It would be almost impossible to name them individually, but they know who they are…

Barbie

In the Beginning

Just the Facts: Alzheimer's disease is the 6th leading cause of death in the United States overall and the 5th leading cause of death for those aged 65 and older. It is the only cause of death among the top 10 in America without a way to prevent it, cure it or even slow its progression.

"In my professional opinion it will be within the next 12 hours." The words were as direct, as she was kind; as honest as she was compassionate. When Brittany, the visiting hospice nurse, spoke them, it was as if there wasn't anything to doubt or question. After all, observing people during their last moments in this life was part of her job and if there was anyone more qualified to make the call… we couldn't think of one. So there we had it. Someone finally had the courage to tell us what we knew, but what no one else would say. Imagine, as many have, that they had only 12 hours left with their mother. That morning as Dave and I stood over her as she lay in bed at her home, we were asking all the questions on our minds, especially because we all wanted to be with Mom when she stepped from this world into heaven. That was our goal, to hold her hand and pass her on. We were told by Brittany that Mom would go when she was ready. She may even go when we weren't in the room with her. Brittany questioned whether Mom might have any unresolved issues that I needed to talk to her about.

It was the day after "Hosanna Day" and the beginning of Passover. For Christians the world over, this was a day of particular significance, and if there was one thing my mother was…it was a devout Christian. I knew Mom would hold off until God's perfect calendar, where the Old and New Testament met. Not on Easter, the following Sunday, but today when the blood of the Old Covenant met with the Lamb of God, the real Passover. This was her "white as snow" day, I just knew it. That was on March 25th , 2013, at approximately 11am. Mom's time of death was marked at 12:01 am March 26th , 2013.

This is our story, the story of our journey through Alzheimer's.

Alzheimer's is a plural illness that doesn't only take the one who has it. It consumes the ones who live with and care for that person. It is the elephant in the room, creating denial, fear, confusion, panic and ultimately grief and loss. It is the illness that takes the very mind of its victim and which eventually subdues the body's ability to control itself. It is sad beyond belief. As a daughter I watched as it not only took my mom, but almost broke my dad.

It was his decision to do what he felt was right. For my dad, the words, "hard," "stressful," or "difficult" were never a consideration. It was his pact with Mom to keep her home, to not place her in assisted living away from him. It was love "until death do us part" in its purest form. Intimate, devoted, and uncompromising love; the kind that doesn't relinquish the care and responsibility of someone else in their greatest need. In spite of everything, it was a beauty to be witnessed over and over again.

Love is eternal in the heavenly realm. It is the hope that motivates and carries us. Mom knew this love. She persevered in it and clung to it even when the early years of her marriage were riddled with mistrust, foreboding and suspicion. Those days were certainly troublesome. They threatened to divide her family and tear her world apart. In those days, I am not sure Mom was thinking so much about love being patient. She did not delight in its adversity. Her children were mean, not understanding her turmoil. Her friends abandoned her, not respecting her loyalty to her husband. No, those years were the days when unknown to her, God was carrying her. Dad lived with his own quilt. He likely is living with it still. But oh, how the last 25 years changed all of that. Throughout that time, he nurtured, sheltered, supported and fed her. Essentially, he poured himself out for her. There is nothing he wouldn't have done.

"Husbands, love your wives, even as Christ also loved the church, and gave himself up for it."
Ephesians 5:25

This truth doesn't negate life's dangerous and bumpy road we all face daily, with circumstances beyond our control, but it was his truth and she was his whole world. She loved everything about him, too. She knew she was spoiled. Love had become not self-seeking, but one body, with each more anxious about the others welfare than their own.

Mom and Dad had known one another since they were 12 years old. They were married when they were both 18 years of age. Many would say they were too young. Yet, when Mom died it was just short of 56 years of marriage. My husband and I saw that marriage in the end and it was something to be envied and revered.

I met my husband after years of bad relationships where commitment was a byword; responsibility and fidelity, a joke. I will never forget having a cup of coffee with him. I recall looking across the table and witnessing in his eyes, devotion and integrity, something I had not intimately seen before. It was not a young man's lust, it was honor. I remember thinking he would swim across the ocean for me. He was an answer to my own admonition to find a good person, one who works, one who has morals, and one who sees beyond past mistakes.

We met in 1997, during the days of the Clinton-Lewinsky scandal. We would have lunch listening to "Rush Limbaugh" on the beach in his red pickup truck. Rush was one of his favorite people. Dave, my husband now, admired him and if ever there was a man he wanted to meet it was Rush. This scandal was a turning point for me. It was in processing the events of this shameful embarrassment that I pondered much in the department of morality. Perfect. Now I would need to address my own sketchy life choices. Having worked in the restaurant/hotel business much of my adult life, I realized, looking back, that I went with the flow and saw the world through some "sophisticated" set of values which I just accepted and participated in.

The foolishness of this scandal became personal to me. The Presidents, many said, "…always had affairs. This was just more public and more heavily scrutinized; especially by his detractors…" It was, "none of our business." Well, it was my business. This was my President who now had been so stupid, undignified, and selfish, allowing this country to be divided in a way no one ever had. In having these discussions with Clinton defenders, I was entering the arena of political sophistry which, to this day, puts my stomach in knots.

On the positive side, this scandal spawned an entire variety of discussions and raised some serious questions. What about the rest of us? When would we grow up and stop being juvenile? At what point does one quit making excuses and accept full responsibility for one's own actions? It reminded me some of grown parents smoking pot and ignoring that their teenagers were smoking it, too. You can just hear the whiny excuses. "It never hurt me, I've turned out fine, and so what's wrong with it?" Addictions and justifications come in many different forms. Somewhere inside of me, Mom had instilled a code of worthiness.

Although I had hidden many a sin and disgrace from her, I knew when it came to morality, she was a Saint.

I remember calling Mom when I was going to get a divorce, crying because I wasn't as strong as her. I did not have the perseverance she had, which was a very embarrassing reality. Today, I own that perseverance and I am blessed.

Yes, the Clinton era made a difference and forced me to ponder my own rebellious behavior, along with its effect on others. Fortunately, I landed in a place I could be proud of.

"Therefore confess your sins to each other so that you may be healed. The prayer of a righteous man is powerful and effective"
James 5:16

My real grown-up relationship with Mom began almost 13 years ago…at the end of the school year. We, (my children and I), finished packing our possessions into a rented moving van in Castine, Maine. We drove to Portland, Maine, to move into our new house which involved my marriage to Dave. I have so many memories.

At this point, Dave and I had been together for almost three years. He proposed to me on his knee in front of the kids on Valentine's Day. From the beginning, fights and all, it has been a good love, a loyal love, a passionate love. Having both come out of bad marriages, it is nothing short of a miracle how we worked through the garbage and strongholds of our past. When we decided to marry, we also determined that moving to Portland was where we wanted to be. Dave owned a house there, and it was to become our home. His Mom was only a few short blocks from us and my parents lived in Bridgton, Maine, a 45 minute drive. We felt we should be near them. We also felt that the isolating community of Castine, while beautiful, was not where we wanted the kids to be. They had had the safety, the wonder of the woods, and the freedom of the ocean in their younger years. As they entered their teen years, we foresaw problems coming for them. We have never looked back nor regretted this decision.

Yana, my oldest daughter, was a sophomore in high school, Tracy was in junior high, and Nate was in 3rd grade.

I recall all of this to put my mom's illness in a time frame. That summer, Mom and I bonded on a whole new level.

Mom always wished and desired that we would all live "next door." You know what I mean. "Need some sugar?…" next door. "Help with your homework?..." next door. "Hello Grammy,

Hello Grampy! Hugs and kisses…" next door! We weren't next door, but we were most definitely closer, and she was happy.

I remember moving mine and Dave's stuff into the house while he was off to sea. Dave's occupation as a Marine Engineer required frequent travel, and at that time he was employed by an offshore drilling company which was drilling off the coast of Nigeria. Mom took all his pots and pans and all my pots and pans and matched them. She separated anything that was a double so we could drop them off at the Salvation Army. What fun we had, and what a huge help she was. Cleaning blinds, organizing, and looking at special places in the house in which she could imagine how we'd decorate for Christmas. Where I saw a problem, she saw the solution.

Mom was very excited for another reason, too. That summer, she had planned a road trip for the two of us. Never had we done a girls' time of travel, and she was thrilled. She thought of everything, including money, my privacy, and the bus schedule. Even now, when I look back, my heart is full of insight as I consider her lovely face of anticipation. This was a big deal for Mom. She was leaving "Daddy", as she called him, and going off on an adventure with her daughter. He cried at the Greyhound station as he blew kisses toward us, as the bus drove away.

Our trip included going to Pennsylvania to see her mom, joining up with my Aunt Donna Rae, her beloved sister in New York City, then going to Atlantic City to stay at Aunt "Donnie's" apartment.

Reflecting on this trip fills me with smiles. Both my Aunt Donnie and my mom tucked their money in odd places; pinned inside of clothes, separated in pockets and "secret" zippers in purses. A dollar here, a dollar there. Mom preplanned tips for the drivers, and tips for the restaurant wait staff. Here a tip, there a tip. In my younger years, I'd have spurned the idea of my "dingbat" heritage, but now I consider it a badge of honor.

These women loved one another with a quirky devotion and funniness. They talked, laughed, hugged and read prophecy. Hal Lindsey's <u>The Late Great Planet Earth</u>, was Donna Rae's favorite book. Nothing was on their radar but sisterhood. Aunt Donnie was so delighted to show us New York City. She took us to a diner right outside of the bus station, she walked us up Broadway, 5Th Ave, Central Park, Times Square and showed us how to "walk in and out" of Tiffany's. It was a wonderful day!

My husband and I have gone to New York City many times since. We have gone with my brother Scott, with and without our kids. Each time, we have been fortunate to add to our bank of memories, (always making time to visit ground zero and pay our respects to the victims who lost their lives that fateful day). I never grow tired of the Big Apple, but that first memory, the summer of 2000, holds a very special place in my heart.

Donna Rae lived in Atlantic City, so after New York, the three of us bussed to her apartment. Her apartment was in a Jewish Tower. While she was a Christian, she was also a volunteer for the Israeli army. My Aunt, along with me and Mom, had a fondness for the Jew, Israel, and the "apple of Gods eye." The tower was, in many ways, an eyesore, located at Donald Trump's Taj Mahal. This Jewish community wouldn't sell out, so Mr. Trump built around it at the driveway entrance. I remember thinking how cool it was to walk out the apartment hallway straight onto the Taj roof, down to the boardwalk lining the beach. Once outside, you could see casinos, shops and food vendors galore, with people everywhere. I would go into the casino at night and play the nickel machine, while Mom and Donnie walked near me, chit-chatting in hushed girly voices.

They stood so close, arm and arm. Nothing could separate their valued time together.

Mom and I also went to Pennsylvania to see her Mom, "Sal" as most called her. I was never fond of my grandmother. To this day I don't know why, but Mom loved her. My mother was never anything but kind to her. That was just my mom. She loved Grams apartment with her kitchen in her usual "red." My grandmother always had a red kitchen. It was a signature of hers.

My mom was infinitely patient with her mom. My grandmother was unruly in conduct and behavior when we were there. She actually chased Mom by car when my mother left to come back to our hotel. Mom had gotten us a room for my privacy. As I look back, I am amazed at how much Mom cared for me. She had given me "down" time, as she understood I was not the people-person she was.

What we didn't know then but were soon to find out was my grandmother; her mother, had Alzheimer's.

For the next few years, Mom and Dad drove faithfully to visit my grandmother in Pennsylvania, and then to Connecticut, where Donnie eventually landed near her own children in assisted living. Both died from Alzheimer's related deaths. Gram was 89 and Donna Rae was 71. My mom was 73 when she eventually passed on.

After Donnie's death, Mom never stopped grieving. She missed her sister with a painful longing. As a result, and perhaps in an effort to fill her desperate void, she began to view me, less as a daughter and more as her friend. As time progressed, she shared more and more intimate details of her life with me.

All that Donnie had been to her, I now was. How thoroughly sacred were my last years with her. I had become her sisterhood fortress.

Who am I
In this body no longer 20
In this mind no longer angry
In this soul no longer lonely
Who am I
With pleasure in my hands…pounding at my heart, as I

touch her book with His Words.
Who am I
That her joy, her hold to sanity, her love would give it to me?
Who am I
As I consider their lives, their challenges, their exhausting
pain, their birth from the same womb…their mother.
Who am I
In their shared victory as they join together, I join too in …
eternal praise.
Who am I
That my knees would bruise, that like them my voice would
groan, my eyes would tear, my heart would ache for them,
that came from us…
Who am I
That I would laugh like them, get distracted like them, and
see them in the mirror.
Who are you?
One day like us will you be; your eyes, spirit, and soul with
solid resolve on Him? Will you like me finally reflect with
fluttering joy and a great big smile? Will you touch that book
and experience His Words as you recognize our notes and
become one with us….

Written by Georgie Ann's daughter after receiving a Bible
once belonging to my
Aunt Donna Rae

Side note: During the early years of their marriage, Dad
served time in prison for white collar crimes. A few weeks before
Mom passed on, she handed him a big bag full of the love letters
he had written to her. She said she wanted him to have them now.
He had no idea she even saved them. She did, and she was passing
on all that love back to him before she left. Mom saved every note,
every letter, and every card ever given her. I wouldn't refer to her
as a hoarder by any means. It's just that people meant that much to
her. Our words mattered. It is heartwarming today, to funnel
through all of her paper.

" before I close-I love you-miss you-adore you-and cherish
you"
Love Daddy
"Hon I love you very much and you are on my mind and so
close I can almost touch you"
Love Daddy
"Well that's all about all for now. My love is with you and
will always be"
Love Daddy

Excerpts of letters written to Mom from Dad while in prison
in the 70's.

Technology, Two Masters, Two Teachers, Two Daughters and Love...

Just the Facts: Alzheimer's disease isn't an immediate descent into forgetfulness. Instead, it is a progressive decline in cognitive function that erodes memory and reduces the ability to perform tasks over a period of several years.

Over the years, I have spent many hours asking myself, "what is she thinking, what must it be like?" How I wanted to open her mind and jump in. I desperately wanted to hear her thoughts, see through her eyes and experience her ever changing world. Dad was always looking for help, a cure, or any way to hold onto her. I, on the other hand, looked for a way to walk with her through what I knew was inevitable. Neither way was right or wrong. He was overwhelmed with the desire to stop this thing that was taking his wife further and further away from him. I was, in some ways, more accepting of it, since in my heart I knew it couldn't be stopped.

"You don't marry someone you can live with; you marry the person who you cannot live without." (James Dobson)

There comes a time when you have to quit asking yourself what it was that you missed, or, "how did this get by me?" Dad and I frequently go back and attempt to capture the moment it all began. Alzheimer's doesn't just appear, and then you die. Diagnosed, misdiagnosed or never diagnosed, Alzheimer's is long and progressive.

I have used Facebook over the years, not so much as a social network, but as a blog, sharing my photos, my life, and my journey. I admit, I also rather enjoy stirring things up, too.

At some point, I began to realize a few things about FB. One, that people write a tremendous amount of foolishness, myself included. Two, that even if I have 200, 300, or more friends, I am not so naive to believe that I actually have that many so called "friends," and neither should you. Three, that to "accept" or "not accept" a friendship request, becomes a huge affront to some. What do I mean by that? People seem to feel that if they request to be "your friend," and you ignore it, then watch out because inevitably there will be, at some time in the future, an alteration or confrontation. FB members act as though others are required to "be" their friend. Not so, my friend. Trust me, if I ignore someone on FB, it seems to become personal.

Everyone I know, aside from my baby brother George, is on FB. My mother-in-law, my brother-in-laws, sister-in-laws, their children, my children, my brother Scott, my sister Sue, cousins and distant relatives, old high school chums, co-workers and church folk. My father, at one time, was on too. I have no doubt, if Mom was able, she would have been a huge fan of this social networking.

Mom introduced me to the computer when she was attending Antioch, to receive her Master's Degree in teaching. We lived in Castine, and I was completely against this technological craziness. She and Dad gave us our first computer so she could show me how to use it and instant message me. She was quite proud of her ability to understand this "new age". She loved MAC's and was always showing me the one at Stevens Brook Elementary School, and all that it could do for her kindergarten class.

I now love my computer for research, photo editing, creating music videos, and to stay in contact with my husband when he is away. I love being able to pop off a quick note by text from my IPhone. I've come a long way since those years. In my opinion, technology rocks!

Technology was the wave of my children's generation. Theirs is the generation it's been tested on, and it has not always gone so well for them. Communication the old fashioned way, by talking, seems to be a thing of the past. We should all be reminded of the grave responsibility we have as parents to "teach them well" in all things. When my son was a young teen, we parents hadn't yet understood the evil that reached out from the internet. The first social networking medium, "My Space," owned by News Corp. at the time, was a site full of porn connections and filth. Thankfully, we caught up, but only after scary encounters with our dear young people. Yes, Satan is alive and well.

Mom's Alzheimer's got so bad that she was no longer able to use technology. It became a battle between her and Dad. He desperately wanted to help her hold on to it. He tried so hard to help her remember her access passwords. He was hoping that if she could just do this, she would be ok. He wrote the passwords and computer directions on pieces of paper, which could be found in a variety of locations throughout their home. Mom wrote everything down on pieces of paper, also, but if it didn't land in her pocket then she would forget where it was.

Originally, Mom had been diagnosed with Primary Progressive Aphasia. Dad worked so hard to help her hold on and maintain where she was in her illness. For years, Dad was helping Mom with this form of dementia, while another one, (Alzheimer's), was medically causing her decline. Did Mom have Aphasia or Alzheimer's? It remains an ongoing question even to this day.

Eventually we received a new gift, Moms laptop. I also took her "Kindle," given to her by my brother, Scott. I was traveling to Israel and wanted to carry a lighter load of books. I knew she needed it to be "out of sight, out of mind," otherwise she would fixate on something she couldn't understand, causing her more frustration and confusion. When she came to my house, I would purposely put the Kindle on the counter to see if she would notice. She would glace at it but she left it alone. I did this type of thing often so that I could observe just how she was.

I talk about computer technology because I'm reminded of 2008, when my daughter, Yana, graduated from grad school. Looking back, I see Mom's illness with more clarity.

Yana had graduated in 2006, from Kenyon College, in Ohio, and Mom wasn't able to make the trip. When she saw the video we recorded, she cried. Not because Yana was a gifted woman, but because Yana lives. Not in the "born again Jesus lives" sense, but in that she survived infancy against almost insurmountable odds. My delivery was less than ideal, and Mom, Dad and my dear friend, Marikay, prayed us through. Both women were literally on their knees in the operating room.

Mom was so proud of Yana. When Yana graduated from UMass, with a teaching degree, Mom was out of her mind with excitement because this trip was only a 2 hour drive to Boston, and she felt she could attend. Yana was now a teacher, like Mom, and they were bonded again. Or so she thought.

2008 just 5 years before Mom passed on. I should have seen it. Today, it is crystal clear.

Mom came to my house with a few paltry photos of Yana. She wanted to make a video as a gift. As I looked through my own photos, disorganized and crazy, I became aware of what a bad Mother I had been. I so ignored picture taking and albums. My world and life, pre-Dave, had been a mess. How could I have not cared enough for my children to do what all Mothers do… marking their lives in photo albums and mementos? I hadn't cared about photos or photography. Pictures were only meant to retain memories, and I knew God, Himself was storing memories in heaven, but on earth memories were bad, plus it was expensive. There was no DSLR or phones with cameras. It was film, and if you were a rotten photographer, as I was, you hated the expense of developing pictures, only to get one decent photo out of a bunch.

That had been me; surviving through a bad marriage, running ragged, raising, and financially supporting my kids, and throwing away memories. Mom was now sitting beside me, all delighted in her idea, and wanting to accomplish this project for her granddaughter. It was an effort of love, and one in which she could not do on her own. Computer, here we go again. Only this time, it's to make our first music DVD and to mark the beginning of my love affair with photography.

I opened the program and gathered all the pictures she had, and all the ones I could muster up from my piles and boxes that I had not yet organized from our move to Portland. Mom was completely incapable of doing anything. She sat and watched and said to me, "You're good! I can't believe how advanced you are on the computer," and, "My eyes hurt, I am not able to keep up." Just like our road trip, I recall her charming face of anticipation, smiling, and giving me the "thumps up" sign. Days later, Mom was thrilled. I put my own twist on it, and made it personal, then gave Mom the co-credit. She loved it.

Yana, on the other hand, was none too thrilled. In fact, she was downright annoyed. You see, Yana and I had been drawing apart for years. Yana is gay, and we had many a heated argument over this. I didn't just "go with the flow" on this one. Mom and I talked and ached over her. I could reconcile this in the sense of "dysfunctional upbringing" or the worldly "live and let live" value, but I was not, and am not able to reconcile it, Biblically. So, though I felt then, and still do feel that I loved and supported Yana in her endeavors, we were becoming estranged over this and it was painful. Yana felt our DVD was just a ploy of sorts, meant to make me feel good about something… exactly WHAT, was beyond me.

I wanted to scream at her, "…what mother feels good enough, what mother feels they did enough, what mother truly feels they can "take the credit" for anything? No, a mother is not a boastful job, and by the way, this was your grandmother's idea."

In my experience, there does exist a salacious agenda that permeates the country. It distorts much that is worthy for its own progressive evolutionary religion that, "anything is good and right." That is not true. As crazy as the fundamental Christian may be to some, so is fundamental liberalism to me. Today liberalism is often, "my way or the highway."

I'm not having any of it. I will take the highway I chose, thank you very much.

Yana walked right into this environment. I was somewhat familiar with it. As a recovering alcoholic, of many years, I had seen the fringes of it back in the early 80's. It made me uncomfortable then, and it made me really uncomfortable for her. I found it a huge insult that some would have the audacity to accuse me of not loving my daughter because I happen to disagree with them and/or her. Who gives anyone this majestic power?

Love is not some blind loyalty to a cause, it is love, no matter what. I love my children period. I do not have to change what I believe in, as a Christian, in order to do so.

Love is not progressive. It is eternal and fixed.

Mom felt strongly about God and His Word, though she was meek in her evangelism. She told me that she and Yana had walked the beach together, and that she, Mom, gathered the courage to tell her a bit about how she felt.

Mom and Dad weren't well to do by any means. Neither was I, especially when the kids were young. After Dave and I married, he generously provided our income although we are still modest today, by many standards. Yana went off to Kenyon College in Ohio. It is a very expensive college, with many well to do students. She did this by her own academic achievement, receiving a large scholarship and help from her grandfather, Larry. Her friends were mostly upper class, either economically, or academically. Her partner attended Smith College, in Massachusetts.

By and large, her friends treated me with polite distain whenever our paths crossed. I got the feeling that my conservatism and Christianity were a punch line. I think that while she was in college, I was even more of an embarrassment. To her and her friends, she was a victim and I was a wolf.

Yana once brought a college friend home, who stayed with us for a day, and then suddenly left, unannounced. I was flabbergasted. I felt then, and still do, that it was a shocking economical thing for this girl. Yana said her friend thought I was mean. Mean? I wasn't cool as a parent of teens, I got that. When our kids were younger, Dave and I would stalk them to be sure they were, where they said they would be. We regularly drove the neighborhoods checking the parent paranoid safety box.

Yana's gayness certainly made things more complex, like girls sleepovers. What to do... what to do? Also, I think there is an elusive social snobbery in life, which begins early on in young people. It is so easy to stumble over what's really important. The coolest place is the one with the unsupervised cellar, the swimming pool, the one with the progressive parent, the parents with money, anything to shine as a badge to avoid embarrassment at all costs. I don't know how to word this nicely. Sometimes as adults, we are very shallow and we teach this to our children.

My parents were none of that. Mom pursued a higher education later in life, but only as a means to do what she loved; to teach children. I never tired of my parents' generosity. They seemed to have endless yard sale gifts in hand. Mom's beloved 25 cent book finds, their meals, simple and good, their home décor tied together by antiques, imagination, and fun. They were smart, but not sophisticated in the elitist worldly way. They understood their roots, and they were proud of them.

Much of Mom's jewelry and clothing consisted mostly of second hand store purchases, but she was always well put together. She was thoughtful in her frugalness, and she had an uncanny ability to be "fancy" and cute. It was not until after she died, that I even knew she owned pearls… real pearls. Mom's favorite was a Bakelite set. She wore it in a beautiful orange necklace, earrings and bracelet. Like my grandmothers signature red kitchen, I think of this set as Moms signature jewelry. I have not been able to bring myself to wear them yet. When Dad could afford it, he always bought her pretty things. He had lovely and rich taste.

I was never embarrassed by them, or their environment. Dad asked me once if I was embarrassed, with tears in his eyes. God's honest truth, he asked me. I was so shocked at the question I could hardly reply. My own eyes welded up, and I hugged him. "No," I said, "never."

You see, love is love no matter what. It is not tied to some social elitism. It is not being a communitarian or a worker for Habitat for Humanity. While it is admirable to be kind, kindness does not equal love. Love is not something to be worn so others can see, and make us feel all good inside. It is not some popular new program where we give each other back slaps. Love is not about "self," and who you know, or even what you do. Love is a bond that doesn't credit itself. It's about hanging tough and seeing past all that the world values, along with all of the false pride that is at its core.

I loved my mom and I love my dad, not because of what they could give me, or because of what they had. I loved them because I just loved them. It's so simple.

"And this is love: that we walk in obedience to his commands. As you have heard from the beginning, his command is that you walk in love."
2John 1:6

I was the biggest recipient of Mom's love, especially when I was living with disappointment over the rebellion of both of my daughters. Yana barely talked to me, and Tracy ran off from Jerry Falwell's Liberty University, to "shack up" with a high school sweetheart, who was then living in San Diego. He was in the Navy. Yana, the constant liberal in our family, must have laughed until her toes hurt.

Amazing, how daughters can become great friends when they are mad at their mother. Mom, in spite of her illness, hugged me and talked. She tried, as was her way, to fix it. She hurt for me, having herself, been estranged from my younger sister for well over 15 years. She understood the pain. A mom can experience a sense of abandonment, as well as a child. I suppose the difference is that moms must keep their chins up. They must always be ready with open arms when restoration calls. A mom needn't accept a behavior that is outside of their realm of acceptance, but they must continue to love and forgive when necessary.

I have searched my heart and soul for what I believe. And yes, I will give an account before God. In the meantime, we have not refused or withheld ourselves, or home, from either Yana or her partner.

Tracy eventually married Roger, at city hall in San Diego. Dave and I flew out to surprise them. We were not going to miss her marriage vows.

"So God created man in his own image, in the image of God he created him; male and female he created them."
And they lived happily ever after…your little face so dear so sweet, tucked away in a blanket with dolls and animals beside you, a couch surrounding your tiny body, your hair messed and fallen.
I dance, I climb, I jump. My fingers reach and point, a hand is formed in a picture of beauty, stretching out in a ballerinas dream.

The music sings the same song in different words "Beauty and The Beast" or "Snow White" and "Cinderella," in the end always a hug and kiss and then a marriage.

"God blessed them and said to them, "Be fruitful and increase in number; fill the earth and subdue it. Rule over the fish of the sea and the birds of the air and over every living creature that moves on the ground."

The flowers bloom bright and full of color, a pink one, blue and yellow too! Her little feet run across the meadow squealing with the breeze, a dress blowing in the wind. They fall and laugh two voices maybe three. Over the bend the ocean opens up to them as they race towards a tree.

Then God said "I give you every seed-bearing plant on the face of the whole earth and every tree that has fruit with seed in it. They will be yours for food."

And they lived happily ever after.

Just across the field apples, grow, sweet and juicy, tart and hard. Ten pretty fingers reach out and touch, as a bee buzzes past and baskets are carried, up in the sky a bird flies by. You climb up first and I will follow one shoe on one shoe off, her lanky knees moving under her skirt and a sock is left behind.

"And to all the beasts of the earth and all the birds of the air and all the creatures that move on the ground-everything that has the breath of life in it-I give every green plant for food." And so it was.

And she lived her youth…wondering, pondering her days. What lay ahead as the "Sound of Music" played in the background, questioning and resolving. Walking through piles of leafs, a shell on the seashore, and a picture to be made. Tears and laughter, fights and phone calls. A ride in the sky held close by strong hands. The color of aqua and green, waves under toes and sun over sea.

"God saw all that he had made, and it was good."

And they lived happily ever after.

Her room is quiet now filled with memories. A picture hangs with a friend, a sister, and a brother, her grandmother sits on her bureau. A knitted poem reads "Sweet innocent child

so precious and dear" while a song sings "Take my-self and I
will be ever only all for thee."
"This is now bone of my bones and flesh of my flesh"
Her mother cries as she looks out the kitchen window
beyond. Heart of my heart now lost in the storm. The
wedding tent has been taken down, the guests have gone
and a beautiful white gown hangs in the closet. The bride
and groom have hugged their parents and climbed into a car.
A father gently reaches towards his wife and draws her
close as two arms lift up to wave them off.
"For this reason a man will leave his father and mother and
be united to his wife, and they will become one flesh."

Written for Tracy K by Georgie Ann's daughter and Tracy's
mother

Mom wasn't able to groom herself without help in the last year. I attended to her nails, feet and facial hair. I would visit and sit in a stool in front of her, casually taking care of her womanly vanities. I became aware that she was losing sight of her granddaughters. She had sometimes begun to forget who I was too, but because she saw me often, she always recognized me.

Our conversations were more and more limited. I had long ago kept it simple, but now I was not even bringing up the subject of her granddaughters, for her sake. I only helped her recall what she chose to address. She was, more often than not, remembering her own childhood, which is normal at end of life. Once, when I was grooming her, she looked at me. Yana was heavy on my mind, that day. I had been faithful to keep Yana informed by text and email. We hadn't actually talked for about a year. Mom looked at me. She was so weak, as I held her hand, filing her nails. Out of nowhere, she spoke the words, "Come now, tell Mommy about it." I reached up to her, hugging her frail body and said, "I just really miss her." That was it… Mom still loved all over me. There was nothing she wouldn't do for me, spiritually or emotionally.

Her love would climb a mountain for anyone. Her prayers reached the mountain, of this I am sure.

Mom was a teacher. She loved being a teacher and she loved her students. She taught kindergarten….and did I mention she loved her students? She also loved her students' parents and families. Not only did she love her students, their parents and families, she loved the people she worked with. Teachers, janitors, staff, the librarian Martha, all of them. That's what she did. She pursued love with a passion. Mom was a love seeker. She sought it, even when love threatened to hurt, crush and batter her. Yes, that was Mom, a love child at heart. She knew love, because she knew God, and He was her very driving force. Mom wasn't any more perfect than any one of us. She made mistakes, she "sinned," and she fell into depression at times, always to bounce back. Not tougher, but softer, and full of even more love.

I have always said I am nothing like my Mom. I was bullheaded… "truth seekers" are more fierce because we generally see in black and white. There is a chasm of difference to "love embracers." People like Mom have people on every corner, just smiling at them in anticipation of a hug, or a kind word. The cashier, Lisa, at Rite Aid, the counter workers at the grocers, even the guys at the transfer station, Kenny and Val, all smiled and waved at Mom.

She knew them, their stories their children and families, and she always displayed warmth and goodness toward each and every one.

Mom never thought about love she just did it…she walked in love and she was fiercely obedient to the object of love: God Himself.

Side note: At the beginning of January, 2013, Yana and her partner brought home baby infant twin boys out of the foster care system hoping to legally adopt them. They are beautiful. Yana did reopen the door between us, shortly before we lost Mom. She and her partner have welcomed us into the boys' lives, and we are very thankful. Mom never knew about this but I am sure, like all children and babies, Mom would have loved them completely, too.

We are also restored to Tracy and Roger, and are very pleased to have a son-in-law so devoted to family.

During Mom's last week, while she was in a coma, Yana and Tracy were both faithful and loving daughters, calling, texting and even offering to come be by our sides.

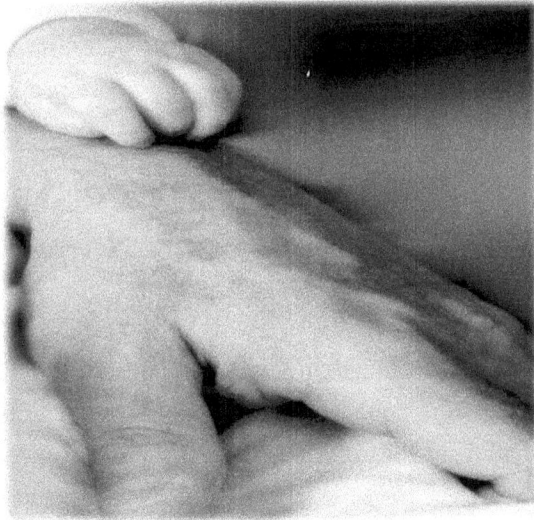

Let's Eat Right to Keep Fit and Treasury's...

Just the Facts: Some live only a few years after diagnosis, while others are still going strong after a decade.

Adele Davis wrote her book, <u>Let's Eat Right to Keep Fit,</u> in 1954. I was born in 1958, which means Mom was a teenager at its first writing. Somewhere in life, Mom discovered Adele Davis and her books. Like Adele, she was an advocate of vitamins in raw natural form, and would often recommend helpful antidotes to whatever ailed you.

I recall, as a youngster, her remedy to prevent a cold was one tablespoon of cod liver oil with a saltine cracker and orange juice to assist with the flavor. We kids plugged our noses during this procedure, to avoid the smell of the cod liver oil. On and off throughout her life, Mom took lecithin, brewer's yeast, (the flake), apple cider vinegar, and honey. To this day, a tablespoon of honey makes me ill. According to Mom, the best cure for a sore throat was warm water and salt which "...works every time."

Like, <u>Let's Eat Right to Keep Fit,</u> Mom fed off of God's Word too. She loved to be challenged intellectually, spiritually, and emotionally, by what He said in The Good Book. She loved the history, patterns, mysteries, and was proud to call herself a dispensationalist, who held tightly to a literal understanding of scripture, whenever possible. God's full council in the 66 books, once handed down for all time, sustained her, and she was a tireless encourager when it came to this precious text.

"All Scripture is God-breathed and is useful for teaching, rebuking, correcting and training in righteousness, so that the servant of God may be thoroughly equipped for every good work."
2 Timothy 3:16-17

I am not really sure when Mom became a Christian. In the last two years of her life, she talked about her childhood, going to church and camp, and Bible study. She expressed some disappointment with her family roots, concerning not being raised in a good Bible believing church. I must confess, I didn't understand some of what she said.

As far as I knew, she had been a Christian all of my life. I know Mom had to become a Christian because that is what the Bible asks for; that one accept, by faith, the free gift of grace from God, and follow Jesus, the Messiah. Mom and Dad had been members of a church early in their marriage, but it was a legalistic church, and eventually they became let down by its requirements. Legalism is defined as adding to Gods word, things that aren't there. Many churches do that, and it can be one of the greatest deterrents for honest God seekers. As a result, we "kids" were not raised as Christians, but we always had a sense of its presence. I intuitively knew that knowing Jesus was important.

I thought I had become a Christian in 1982, but as I look back, I am not sure. It was in 1982, when I was recovering from alcoholism, that I turned my will and life over to God. Jesus was the only God I had heard of, so He was who I turned to. I believed in Him, and I also had several "born again" experiences. Unfortunately, in my heart, I was rebellious and resistant to anything that resembled authority. Jesus was my God, but He had no authority in my life. The key ingredient that was missing, was my own disconnect to "sin" and its abhorrence before a holy God. I could not understand how Adam's sin was passed all the way down to me. The "blood" was an odd thing, "atonement," a foreign language. Needless to say, I lived my life ignoring sin and its grave consequences, not only in my life, but in my children's lives. I didn't grasp the gospel and the real meaning of the cross.

"For the life of a creature is in the blood, and I have given it to you to make atonement for yourselves on the altar; it is the blood that makes atonement for one's life."
Leviticus 17:11

It was on November 3rd, 2003, my son's birthday, while I was doing a women's Bible study in Romans, that I came across these verses;

"For if we have been united with him in a death like his, we will certainly also be united with him in a resurrection like his. For we know that our old self was crucified with him so that the body ruled by sin might be done away with, that we should no longer be slaves to sin because anyone who has died has been set free from sin."
Romans 6:5-7

As I considered these verses, I realized my rebellion, and how I hadn't agreed with God about what sin was… especially my sin. On this day, I once again gave myself, sin and all, to Him. I submitted to a Holy God, understanding for what seemed the first time that Jesus died and became as sin for me. He took all my sin and paid the full penalty at the cross. It was in this one act, that Jesus reconciled me to the Father. I was free, and sin no longer had its grip over me. This was the real beginning of life eternally, and I jumped in, remaining to this day, passionately committed.

Mom had deep faith. Faith was repeatedly her prayer for herself and others. She told me she had prayed for years, that God would increase my faith. At first, I didn't comprehend this prayer of hers, but slowly as I thought about it, the simple profoundness began to sink in. Faith is not about something we can see, touch, or feel. It is a knowing, a dependency, and a resolve. Faith can't be fully explained. The dictionary calls it, "loyalty" or "fidelity" to ones promises. Faith, itself, requires God's strength. It is His fidelity to us, the moment we come to believe in Jesus. We are sealed with the Holy Spirit, although we are incapable of perfect moral sinless fidelity to God. Every day, we compromise, cheat, and ignore the requirement to be holy before Him. It is His faithfulness that gives us strength and hope, over and over again.

*"Now faith is being sure of what we hope for and certain of
what we do not see."*
Hebrews 11:1

Mom was full of the "mustard seed" of faith. She prayed down to the littlest detail. She prayed, with faith, for small things and for big things. As her Alzheimer's got worse, she needed that faith and Gods promise to never leave or forsake her. Unknown to her, God had been preparing her for when she would be helpless and no longer able to care for herself. God had known, too, that He had given her the perfect mate, a man for whom she would have and hold up until her last breath.

Mom and I talked by phone often, as we were always having a mental "aha" God sighting, and had to share it. Nothing was too deep, simple or unimportant. We would both have our Bibles open, each on the other end of our phones. We'd read together and share our thoughts. I remember discovering the Holy Spirit in chapter 4 of the book of Revelation. It was a "Wow" moment for both of us!

Mom, who never tired of taking notes, would write to me, while we sat together in church. She would see or hear something and it couldn't wait. It was one of her "amen" church notes, that opened my eyes to revere the Old Testament. Our Pastor Dave, at the time, was talking about Moses, when Mom passed me a note which said, "Baptism." She was referring to the Israelites passing through the Red Sea, essentially the baptism of a nation. It was then, that I saw that everything in the Old Testament was pointing to Christ and the "fullness of time."

The Bible was a reservoir for us. We never wearied from Gods disclosure to His children. To think that He would choose to use a pattern of written words, and communicate to us in such detail, is awesome.

Mom's gifts from God were compassion and mercy. When she saw suffering in the world, she would take off her jewelry for a time. She would cry and pray. She was generous in her own community, giving gifts and spending time with people. She and Dad would pick a family at Christmas time and go see them, giving as much as they were able. They never bragged, and only barely talked about it.

My gift from God is discernment. Dave, Dad and Mom were infinitely patient and supportive of me, through a painful journey of truth speaking. For Dave and me, our idyllic life in our own home church was rocked upside down, from having upset fellow church members with exposing truths about false teachings, which were permeating our own church. Yet, we grew together as a family in our understanding of God's word.

Again, when I felt abandoned by many in the church,

Mom was a loving force in my life.

As Mom grew worse, I was no longer able to share with her my thoughts on deep theological precepts, apologetics, doctrine or false teachings. I missed our intellectual Biblical dialogue, but Mom was not able to hold on to a lifetime of study, let alone new information. Christian knowledge was drifting off to a place unknown. God graciously shifted my mind to meet her where she now was, and to step into her precarious world as it slipped away. I let go of anything that would distract me from her with a conviction that nothing else mattered.

Honestly, when a person goes through a time of isolation as deep as this, it gives new meaning to the song which says, "You can have this entire world, just give me Jesus." When God moves and draws you to Himself, He never promised it wouldn't be painful, he only promises to walk with us.

Storing up earthy treasures is not what God calls us to do, yet some earthly treasures have eternal value, and I am sure there are many which He smiles on. Mom had a few earthly treasures that were near and dear to her, not the least of which were her books. Mom was a staunch Scofield Bible proponent, having received her first one as a gift from "the kids" and Daddy in 1966. Bible translations were discussed between us as King James became NIV, ESV, and ASV and so on. We had many conversations about rewording and interpretations. She had several other books that she loved and collected to include; C.S.Lewis' Narnia series, Corrie Ten Booms books, The Hiding Place, Tramp for the Lord, and The Silent Years, and Louis La'Mours westerns. She had so many "preacher" favorites, it would be hard to name them all. She was fond of Adrienne Rogers, Chuck Smith, Jimmy DeYoung, and Brother Andrew.

Mom and I enjoyed going to the modern public library, Borders Bookstore. We'd walk to the religious section, stroll, talk and casually turn books around so that the covers would face inward. We did this with books we disagreed with. It was our self-prescribed righteousness, and it gave us great pleasure. We both understood that turning covers away from direct view did not deter ignorance, but it made us feel better, and we thought we were contributing to Kingdom glory. If Christian books of questionable character ended up in our personal home libraries, we decided we would throw them away rather than confuse ourselves with a false prophet's writings, or have one fall into the hands of someone else. For a person who loved books, this was hard for Mom, but she even advised her friends to do the same.

Like her childlike faith, Mom's favorites were children's books. She regularly shared them and gave them away to her once young grandchildren, and to the dozens of kindergarten kids she taught throughout the years. She would endlessly read them aloud, at their homes, in her classroom and in the library. Mom collected books, themes, authors and Bibles. Need a book? Mom had plenty, and she was pleased to share! Mom never came to visit us without a book in hand. In fact, Mom went nowhere without at least one book with her.

After Mom retired from teaching, in 2006, she would volunteer at the Bridgton Public Library. She returned on a regular basis to read to the children. One day Mom was reading aloud and, out of nowhere, she didn't recognize any of the words. She looked out at the young faces and started to cry. Subsequently, Mom was gently escorted out of the room. In a way, it was "goodbye," but she was completely unprepared for it. Mom talked about that incident up until 3 months before she left us. It was a turning point in the depth of her soul, one she could not understand, and one she could not forget.

Whenever Mom talked about her illness, she would say, "when I get better," or, "I am getting better!" There was no sequel to those words, she would just put them out there… "When I get better," followed by a smile. Oh, that smile.

All my Grammy's Books

"The Ox Cart Man" where can you be…beneath the piles before me or hiding near my knee?
Six eyes line the window, hazel and brown, wonder of wonders a bag full of books has just been found.
Here she comes our teacher Grammy…could it be the "Goodnight Moon" or "Free Fall" from leaves high in the tree.
Tiny fingers hold tight the chairs propped looking up the driveway, just twenty minutes longer the day still bright reminds me. "Hello Red Fox" says Eric Carle as she enters

with a bell "The Polar Express" has her excited this story she
has to tell.

Oh joy she longs to share as they sit upon the couch
"Roxaboxen" or "Green Eggs and Ham" if you please, our
Mama s not a Llama they laugh and tease.

Their cat comes up beside them as she reads "Cats here,
cats there, cats and kittens everywhere" while fingers touch
her necklace dangling with beads.

Oh for such a time as this she loved them through and
through "Blueberries for Sal", "Make Way for Ducklings",
"One Morning in Maine" and "Time of Wonder" the cover
written in gold and blue.

For your inquiring, enchanted mind she wrote in '89, moon
snails and spiders are very similar you know for "Chickens
Aren't the Only Ones" where eggs are made to grow.

The funny ones we love "There's a Nightmare in my Closet"
peeping and nestled on the blankets edge "The Napping
House" breaks not my bed when everyone is sleeping.

Should it end not there for further on she goes and here she
comes again with Lewis in tow. By far a favorite each
summer stuffed in her big black purse, the chronicles of
Narnia where Prince Caspian is known to say "I don't like
running away" come jumping off the page.

Yet in another pocket she reveals something new "The Island
of The Blue Dolphin" is torn and tattered too.

She knits you all a snowflake and gives you each a kiss
while her face is singing sagas of the Sacketts' in the west,
L'Mours' historical fictions are sitting on her chest.

Her Shelves appear disordered some would say a
Mess, but hands reach out to touch them her books
above her desk.

She signed everyone one she gave you each child received
her best, a scripture to remind them how wonderfully they're
blessed.

Once asked a person wisely does anyone perceive how much
she loves those written words books "A" to "Z."

Most worshiped within her soul the one the Lord Himself
holds.

She prays the words He's written with each of you in mind,
each one that He has given her His glory may they find...

Written for my mom and my children

Mom would go nowhere without a purse. Although she had a bazillion of them, along with book bags, she ended up enamored with the same purse for the last few years. It was a small beige one. She obsessively put the same things in and out of it to include; her tissues, her dollars, her paper, her glasses, and her two little books. She also kept her keys and phone in her clothing pocket, long after she was able to use either of them, almost until her last days.

Mom ended up keeping only two tiny books with her at all times. They fit nicely in her little purse. They were Scolfield's, Rightly Dividing the Word, and Chuck Smiths, The Soon to be Revealed Antichrist. Mom never read them, for by the time Mom had them in her purse, she really was no longer able to read. Ever faithful to her passion, though, she would pull out one or the other whenever she and Dad were at the doctors or a waiting room. Dad would pick up a loose newspaper in these locations. She would look at him until her mind would light up with remembrance as to her "procedure" in the waiting room. She would reach into her purse and pull out either one of her books, generally holding them upside down incorrectly, and begin to "read."

The first time I witnessed Mom doing the upside down reading, was at my house. As was our pattern, we had books on the ottoman, and we were "God talking." Both of us were snuggled on the couch like girls do, and I picked up a book and was gleaning the index. Mom picked up a book upside down, and she also gleaned. After a few moments, she looked at my hands and book. My eye was slightly glancing at her and my face was smiling. She then looked back at her book, thought for a minute, and turned it over correctly. No words were exchanged, no words were needed. Sweetly, we were silently still "God talking."

Side note: I watched as Mom grew "young" at the end of life. This is similar to the beginning of life. With us it tracked a path, like the child marking new firsts. Mom's last two years marked them in reverse.

Several years ago, I read my Bible all the way through, for the first time. Mom and Dad met me soon after, at Dunkin Donuts, where she presented me with a homemade "crown of victory," cut and put together with colored paper. On it she wrote, "I did it." I had read the good book, and she, true to her kindergarten teacher form, was rewarding me. It was one of the best presents of my life. When Dave made his first read through, it was in the fall of 2011. Mom wanted to make him a crown too, although she kept forgetting how she had done mine. She sat at a table and chair in her front room, trying to accomplish this huge task. Paper, scissors, tape, crayons and pencil. "I can't remember how," she would say, and she really couldn't. Mom reminded me of one of her kindergarten students. Mom, in every way, was a five year old. She smiled like one, the table before her was disheveled like one, and her fingers, body and her dexterity were like one. It was a picture to behold. It was as though we had just opened yet another door closer to the end. With assistance, Mom did make that crown for Dave and he absolutely treasuries it. His crown of victory says, "I love Him."

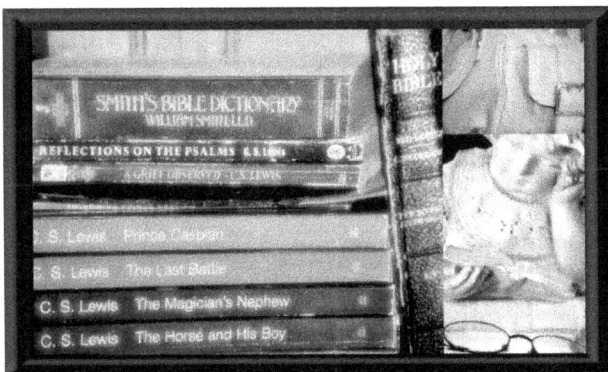

Standing before the Berma Seat there are "crowns" given to believers. These crowns are heavenly rewards for the work we have done for the kingdom. Our "salvation" is not based on our works, it is based on our putting our faith and trust in Jesus for paying our penalty for sin. After we are believers, our work has rewards, and they are given as crowns.

"If any man's work shall be burned, he shall suffer loss: but

"he himself shall be saved; yet so as by fire"

1st Corinthians 3:15

The Incorruptible Crown-1st Corinthians 9:24-27

The Crown of Rejoicing-Philippians 4:1

The Crown of Life-Revelation 2:10

"be thou faithful unto death, and I will give thee a crown of

life."

The Crown of Glory-1st Peter 5:1-4

The Crown of Righteousness-2nd Timothy 1:8

(in part from Jack Kinsella)

Israel and Growing Pains...

Just the Facts: Personality changes become more pronounced by the moderate stage of Alzheimer's. People at this stage may experience hallucinations (seeing and hearing things that aren't there), delusions (mistaken beliefs), paranoia (accusing others of lying, cheating, or stealing from them), and compulsive behaviors (rubbing their hands together over and over or tearing tissues into tiny pieces). They may become angry and even violent, hitting, kicking, or screaming out of frustration.

It was in the late winter of 2011, when Mom and Dad moved to Gray, Maine, nearer to Dave and me. They lived in Avista housing for approximately 7 months, or until that next fall. Dad had moved them, hoping this would be a better location. The housing had about 15 units and some lovely elderly people living there. I thought it was perfect. They had friendly neighbors on all sides. There was a community diner, a recreation room, a laundry facility, and a library just one block away. What more could they need?

Mom and Dad were quick to make friends but eventually they felt like they were constantly being watched… especially Mom, as paranoia set in. It didn't take long for them to realize they had made a big mistake. Mom became increasingly homesick for their familiar surroundings in Bridgton. Almost as soon as they moved to Gray, they were ready to leave.

I was not very pleased, and spoke to my brother concerning this. It was about this time that I started using my brother Scott, who lives in San Diego, California, as a "debrief" family member. We promised we would not keep secrets from one another and that we would be open and transparent, concerning Dad and Mom.

Dave, Scott, and I agreed that, no matter what, we would support any decision that our parents wanted. Their happiness, however inconvenient, was of paramount importance. There were times we would talk out our own frustrations. That was to be expected, and at no time did the three of us ever veer from this pact. Our parents were the most important people in our lives. We loved them, we wanted to protect them, we wanted to honor them, and we would do whatever we could to make their lives easier. We knew we had our tomorrows, but for them, this was their tomorrow that they, and they alone were living. Even though they were doing it on an emotional shoestring, if they wanted to move back to Bridgton, then so be it.

Mom had not yet gone to The Lahey Clinic, nor been diagnosed with Alzheimer's. We were still assuming all of her problems were related to Primary Progressive Aphasia. Nonetheless, we were seeing signs of rapid decline. Mom was becoming more delusional, imagining people who were not there, and accusing Dad of terrible things which were not true. She also became suspicious about her neighbors.

Whenever she knew I was coming, Mom would stand in the window-doorway, waiting and smiling. She talked to me about her perspective, and I would listen. It was becoming harder to follow her thoughts, but I was pretty good at her disjointed conversations. I knew it when she jumped from the here and now, to the past and all the people that had mattered to her (her brother, sister, parents, children and school friends). As she increasingly faded in and out of these subjects, I felt like I was the only one who knew what she was trying to say. At that time, she used her fingers to recall and count. Touching one finger and then another while saying "One, two" or if she was able, "One, two, three, four."

Mom and Dad came to our house often. We would be having coffee and visiting when she would say something aimless, and then look at me and smile, as though I knew what she was talking about. This would be followed by our continued conversation. One minute she would talk about the weather, and the next, her siblings. She was also in the habit of raising her hand for us to "call" on her, as if she was in a classroom setting. If she wasn't "called on," she'd be downright disruptive, interjecting a thought in the middle of an entirely different discussion. Mom would smile while we all remained infinitely patient. Dave and I purposely visited as often as we could for Dad's sake, knowing his days did not consist of "normal" daily chit chat. We all allowed Mom to interrupt with whatever she wanted to say.

She was losing weight, her language, and her grip on reality. I began to intentionally photograph her as I discovered that I was able to witness, in her eyes, the progression of her illness. I would call my brother as the reality overcame me. He, along with Dave, was understanding in my meltdowns and panic. Once Mom reached later stages, the obvious decline of cognitive abilities came in waves as the certainty of her moving further and further away sunk in. I was heartbroken for Dad, who valiantly kept putting one foot in front of the other. Dad never stopped looking for anything to help Mom, to slow the progression or keep her stable. Yet, these days were trying times. Mom was unreasonable and accusatory of Dad. I found myself having to remind him that it wasn't Mom, it was her illness. When she wasn't irrational, Mom knew how much Dad loved her. In fact, she would tell me, "your father would do anything for me." But when she slipped more and more into craziness, it took all his resolve to not fall apart.

It was in the mist of all of this, (in April of 2011), that Dave, me, and our son Nate had our "Angus' Dei" trip. We had wanted to travel to Israel for some time, and decided it was a "now or never" moment. As was Israel's pattern of volatility with her surrounding nations, we felt that it was possible that in the future we might not be able to go. People were a bit worried for us, but we were out of our minds with excitement. We have an enormous fondness for Israel, and as adherents to Bible prophecy, and Gods plan for the Israelis, we wanted to step our feet on the Holy Land. After an immense amount of planning we set off for the airport on April 6th.

Mom and Dad were delighted for us. I felt as though, in some ways, we were doing this with them with our hearts joining theirs in this personal journey. We tried to share every step of the trip. Dad would pull up our pictures from his email to show Mom, and they would both become teary eyed. Mom had given me a map of Israel which had belonged to Donna Rae, who had been there in years past. I took the map and looked at it often. Mom, Aunt Donnie and I were all map fans and to have this map of the Promised Land which once belonged to my favorite Aunt was special, indeed.

I cannot not begin to express the awe of this trip.

Dave, Nate and I bonded in a way that only those who love God and His word can identify with. We stayed in Tel Aviv, at the Park Plaza Orchid, on the beach. We took daily trips from this point of origin, returning at night. We bicycled to Old Jaffa, traveled to the Jordan River, saw Megiddo, walked the old cities of Jesus's day, gazed at Old Jerusalem from the Mount of Olives, cried at the Garden of Gethsemane, stood on Calvary, witnessed the place of Christ's tomb, climbed the stairs to the Rotunda, took pictures of the Chapel of the Franks, toured the Kotel Tunnels, bowed and prayed near the supposed place of the Arc of the Covenant. We talked to Leviticus Priests, covered our heads at the Western Wall and Old City, strolled and smelled the aroma of the Cotton Merchants Market. We were stopped at the entrance to the Dome of the Rock by gun toting guards, soaked in the Negev Desert and the Dead Sea. We toured Masada and the West Bank, went to Haifa, Mount Carmel, Caesarea, and walked the Crusader underground city and the grand gothic Knights Hall. We saw the Roman Theater and aqueducts, Herod's palace, and saw the beauty of Rash Hanikra, along the Lebanon-Israeli border. We talked, and visited with people, whose lives and personal stories were magnificent. It was extraordinary, and unbelievable. We cried, laughed and pinched ourselves at this blessing of a trip. It was intense, historical, and deeply profound for all three of us.

It was, in many ways, the last event in our lives that Mom understood. Our "talkfests" were short lived, because her attention span was limited, but in my heart, I knew she "got it," and so did Dad. They took the time to watch my picture DVD and be amazed. I had purposely put it together to music, which I knew would grip Mom with praises of God. She sat in front of the TV, watching and holding her hand over her heart, as Dad's eyes were attentive with tears.

As selfish as it may seem, I found that this trip brought with it, loneliness afterwards.

We were already well into losing Mom. In many ways, we were still estranged and distant from our daughters. On top of that, we found ourselves questioning what was happening in the church we had been attending. Additionally, my very best friend, Marikay, was consumed with caring for her ailing father and brother. I wanted to talk, and digest what we had seen and done. I wanted to share our moments, but I found that most people were disinterested. I have learned a lot… not only about my own character, but about the character of people in general, since.

I had to work through my own selfishness concerning my dear friend, Mari. It was not until Mom was close to the end that I finally appreciated the unspoken pain Mari had suffered. She cared for her father and brother in the same year, as they left this world to become members of God's heavenly house. She, too, had poured herself out in love and sacrificial giving. She gave to her family everything she had, and then some. Her attentive allegiance was her complete focus. Here was I, her friend, wanting to talk about a trip.

Mari and I have been friends for over 40 years. Not just friends, but best friends, for most of those years. We also knew "God Talk." We both read our Bibles and researched every element of anything we didn't understand until our minds apprehended, what most people just ignore. Yes, Mari was my "go to" friend for everything, and now she needed to put all of her energy into her family. Through it all, I found myself missing her, longing for everything to be normal. It was, for me, a lonely time having just come off of a "high," and a time which I am not proud of.

After Mari lost her father and then her brother, I was sick for her. I knew she had her own mother, children, and family to attend to. But it seemed, for a time, that everything had changed and I began to panic. Now that I am in my own grief, I understand the devotion to family that comes from a time of tragedy and loss. It is the wisdom of God's word that is revealed in the verses;

To everything there is a season,
a time for every purpose under the sun.
A time to be born and a time to die;
a time to plant and a time to pluck up that which is planted;
a time to kill and a time to heal ...
a time to weep and a time to laugh;
a time to mourn and a time to dance ...
a time to embrace and a time to refrain from embracing;
a time to lose and a time to seek;
a time to rend and a time to sew;
a time to keep silent and a time to speak;
a time to love and a time to hate;
a time for war and a time for peace.
Ecclesiastes 3:1-8

Once Marikay had moved through some of her grief and we were well into Moms final months, she was a sweetheart, sharing her experience, strength, and hope with me. Marikay cheered me on through some of our most difficult days, having lived through them, herself. I love her so much and I am so grateful for God's faithfulness in our friendship. It is a friendship that He, Himself, has protected, and has brought through many fires. It is the pureness of two women growing and being nurtured in the will of God. When we first met, I was only 12 years old but I know we never imagined how far He would bring us, or that He would draw us both to Himself through the Cross.

When Mom was well enough, she would read from her Bible and use Jimmy DeYoung's web site for his daily devotions. She would send me his link, as she was always having deep illuminated moments from what he had to say. Jimmy DeYoung has been a friend to Israel as long as anyone. He has a web site called "Prophecy Today." He has written many books, does a weekly radio show, church conferences and is a regular on Brannon Howse's Worldview Weekend broadcast. Jimmy has a very distinct voice and we both enjoyed listening to him. Soon after our return from Israel, Mr. DeYoung came to Portland, Maine, to speak at the First Baptist Church. Dave and I invited Mom to come with us to see him. By this point, Mom had forgotten so many things from her Bible study. She had forgotten who Jimmy was, but she knew whatever we were doing was "big," and she thought that if she went and saw him, it would help her to remember. We sat directly in front of Mr. DeYoung in the second row, so Mom was practically on top of him. She smiled a lot. I could tell though, in looking at her face, she didn't comprehend what was actually being said.

Mom was so pretty that night, dressed in a white dress I had bought her and which she was eventually cremated in. Dave took a picture of us that I came across recently. I cried as I saw her in that dress. Who would have ever known? In spite of her not recalling all she had hoped for, we had a wonderful time, and it was very special to know that Jimmy DeYoung had spiritually helped to sustain Mom all these years in his teaching of end times and prophecy.

That was August 6th, 2011. We had been in Israel, 4 months prior. With all that was going on, it was a distinctly interesting time for us. Little did we know at that time, we would lose her 20 months later?

Side note: Mom delighted in our son Nate. When she would see him, she'd walk up and talk about anything she could think of referring to God, as though it was a new introspective thought, or one he had never heard before. I can see him, standing tall above her with her little body, eye glasses and hands moving in delight. Nate would look at me. I knew he couldn't follow a single thing she said but he would affectionately hug her and grin. Mom would open the ever present Bible, sitting on our kitchen counter. She'd point to a scripture and tell Nate all about the thoughts she had that day on the verses. Often, she couldn't find the exact one she'd read, but that mattered not. She had much she was trying to teach him. He was her grandson, and a ready audience. Nate had been homeschooled and taught in the ways of God. His grandmother adored him along with all of her grandkids.

Mom always felt she had a unique understanding into each of her grandchildren. Perhaps it was her kindergarten teacher background or perhaps it was just that being a grandmother affords you wisdom and insight. With Nate, Mom was able to discuss her favorite subjects; God and the Bible. There is, indeed, a rare bonding that happens around abiding in the truth.

I am not able to understand how shutdown people are on the topic of God, His Word, and The Cross. For all that can be "bright" in many people, they still seem to be disconnected, intellectually and thoughtfully, about a theme so rich and mentally challenging. People's eyes gloss over, they exchange glances, and they smirk. I recently heard Brannon Howse talk for an hour on the "Tower of Babel" and the biblical and historical background of that event and how it relates to the church today. The richness of history he offered up was mind boggling. When the Bible is presented in a "connect the dots" way, it is fulfilling… not only spiritually, but mentally.

God is an infinite subject and the word of God is beautiful, academic and stimulating.

It is the whole story...

"Hatikvah"
The National Anthem of Israel

As long as the heart, within, A Jewish soul still

yearns, And onward, towards the ends of the east,

An eye still gazes toward Zion;

Our hope is not yet lost, The hope of two thousand

years, To be a free people in our land, The land of

Zion and Jerusalem

Doctors, Road Trip and Realty

Just the Facts: I have aphasia (uh fay zhuh). It's a communication problem. My intelligence is intact. I am not drunk, on illegal drugs or mentally unstable. Give me time to communicate. Speak simple and directly to me. Do not shout- it doesn't help. Ask yes or no questions.

It has been only since 2006 that Dad and I began to notice a problem with Mom. As of this writing, that's 7 years ago. Dad and I rehash the years and are struck by how quickly they went by. For anyone who has lived through this, they can well understand that even today, (4 months after we lost Mom), we are both just worn out. Especially Dad. How do you go from full speed ahead to full stop, without experiencing some depression, exhaustion and a sense of "now what do we do?" Both of us "putsy" and dabble in projects and activities. Slowly, we are going through Mom's personal belongings to include clothing and her plethora of pictures, cards, letters and paper.

I write, obsess over photography, go to work, and generally attempt to clean my house, pay bills and keep my family members content. But there is an ongoing ache and restlessness to my day. A person has but one Mother, so in losing her, I have nothing else to compare it to. I do not know if this grief is part of a normal process or if it is compounded by having co-supported Dad through the physical and mental insidiousness of Alzheimer's.

Mom made us laugh and smile often but in the last year, her deterioration was so erratic that we both felt powerless to keep up. As Moms affliction progressed, her daily routines and patterns were very unpredictable. The doctors did their best to help and suggest things. They made medicine adjustments and were thoughtful to both my parents. Unfortunately, unless a doctor walks directly through this fire, they too are quite ineffective to do more than listen and offer medical advice. For those caretakers on the front lines, we often marvel at how feeble even the "pros" seem to be in actually knowing this illness. For us, Mom's Alzheimer's was like living in a virtual mental ward during the last months. How one dear, lovely, tiny lady could so unknowingly cause as much havoc as she did, is one of the many fascinations and marvels I am left with contemplating today.

For seven years, my parents seemed to go nonstop to doctors and medical professionals. It was one thing after another. It would be an over simplification to refer to those years as elderly hypochondria. There were real medical issues that both my parents needed treatment for. Considering that, along with Mom's cerebral malady, and Dads vigilant advocacy on her behalf, they spent a tremendous time at appointments.

Mom had several eye surgeries for cataracts, but she also had glaucoma. The amount of pressure within this eye went up at different times and her eye doctor would have to slit the eyeball to relieve the buildup. Whenever she had this procedure done, she would have to be at the doctors the following morning to be checked. One time, following this procedure, she decided that rather than go home to Bridgton, she would stay with me and have a girl's night. Dad then would come to our house early in the morning and we'd all go back to the eye doctor together.

Mom slept in my bed, but in the wee hours of the morning, I became aware that she was no longer beside me. I got up as she was coming back from the bathroom. I don't recall all that she said but she wasn't herself. She told me she felt very sick. I helped her get dressed and down the stairs. It took her a very long time. She sat on her behind and slowly, in a seated position, went one step after the other. It was just awful. I was so worried and almost called an ambulance. I called my father, instead. I assisted her out to our car just as Dad drove in. The three of us then rushed off to her eye doctor, Dr. Libby.

I have never understood exactly what happened but to this day, I know it wasn't good. Although every doctor has said she didn't have a stroke, I'm still not sure. I have always felt sick about this incident and when Mom would bring it up she would remark that I "saved" her. She would brag to me about what a stupendous job I did. All of her love and bluster toward me has never taken away the guilt I have felt at this. I can't help but think it contributed to her future problems.

As a result of all of her eye problems, Mom was very sensitive to light and the sun. She was constantly having vision troubles.

It was a short time after this daunting experience that Dad and I began to notice something wrong with her speech. Dad approached me to find out if I was noticing what he was. Dad thought that perhaps she had something neurological going on. He did think, fearfully, that maybe she had Alzheimer's, since it had run in her family. Eventually, Dad made an appointment at Maine Medical Geriatrics Center. Mom had a slight amount of testing done and over time we met for a clinical consultation. We sat in a room where the doctors and assistants explained that Mom had, what is called "Primary Progressive Aphasia."

What a relief, it's not Alzheimer's!

Aphasia is not that well-known and poor Mom could never remember what she had. She was always forgetting the word "aphasia." She wrote handwritten, personal notes, over and over again. Dad also made for her a business card size "helps" card, which she kept in her pocket to show people. Essentially, this card explained the following:

I have aphasia (uh fay zhuh). It's a communication problem. My intelligence is intact. I am not drunk, on illegal drugs or mentally unstable. Give me time to communicate. Speak simple and directly to me. Do not shout-it doesn't help. Ask yes or no questions.

Mom was quite adorable at using this even when it seemed unnecessary. Her concern was that someone would treat her badly if they didn't understand she wasn't crazy. She would just pop that card out and hand it to people for no apparent reason.

Dad searched, high and low, for help with this form of dementia. There were all kinds of Alzheimer's support groups, but few for aphasia existed. He found a speech pathologist that specialized in this area. Steven Belanger, SLP, had a practice here in Portland and he also mediated a support group with others of like condition, along with their spouses and family members. Mom and Dad loved the people and I was overwhelmed with relief when I went. To sit in a room of bright people, afflicted with aphasia, and witness their struggles, victories, common laughs and jokes was a special pleasure. Most people typically have this brain disturbance from a stroke but in Moms case, no stroke was diagnosed. Some aphasia, as I understand it, is an atypical form of Alzheimer's. Like Alzheimer's, there is no cure. Aphasia means "speechlessness." Aphasia is a progressive language and brain disorder. Its only treatment is speech therapy which can help a patient to some degree. Dad lined Mom up with plenty of that. He also continued to help her maintain, and hold on to her piano lessons.

Mom had taken up the piano and loved Kim, her teacher. Mom always wanted to play the piano and in her later years, she was an eager student. This musical release gave her great joy. Kim was more than a teacher, she was a friend and fellow Christian. She stayed with Mom, even when Mom could no longer read or play. Kim loved Mom and to her credit, Kim kept her as a student until 4 months before we lost her.

Speech therapy, group therapy, new eye glasses, sun glasses, hats to shade her eyes, note cards, piano… whatever she needed, Dad made sure to provide it for her.

Mom, true to her teacher training, took all of her "assignments" earnestly. As we have gone through the boxes and folders she kept, it's apparent that Mom made notes and wrote, constantly. Anything she heard or thought of got written down on sticky tabs. If the news was on, the news was written. If someone called, their conversation was written. If she went somewhere, her trip was written. Mom took seriously the idea of staying mentally active with language. She played card games and scrabble with Dad. She was engaged with her illness. She attempted to read about it and she didn't just sit back in a state of apathy. She was proactive.

In reading through Mom's mountain of notes and note books, I find myself laughing aloud at how amusing I find her thoughts. What she told herself, and attempted to remember is quite remarkable. Mind you, Mom was always good with grammar and spelling. In reading her papers, I am struck by her condition. I saw it when she was still using the computer and would send me an email, but now I have a second firsthand look. Below, is Moms writing about a childhood memory. I have transposed spelling and sentence structure as she wrote it, to give an example of what was happening to her.

Kids Playing Outside, 1955
I am one of them
I called Mother to watch me race me with no hands.
I don't know what was because I was asleep.
I now I Ride Race with my hands.
We had a river on I side of the road and homes mostly on the side on the other side.
My neighbor and our had driveways far enough to play races both come, coming from the river side and houses side.
There were mud puddles Racing both way Racing through the puddles with no hands!
Mother was in the house on the away fromest from the river.
I yelled away for as loud as I could I wanted to show-off Hey!! Mother looking at this.
As Mother was running to the me on the as I bike, with no hands, no notice that I was going through much to toward the bank while Mother yelling for me to stop!
When I "got awake from the falling, as I fell knocked out.

I had some bruises, but they were ok. But my parents, after they know they I was going to be k, were not ok--- until they had a long preaching.

Written by sweet Georgie Ann approximately 2010

Mom drew closer to God, albeit in childlike simplicity. She began to say, "people always ask me, 'Georgie how you do it?'… God's got it" she'd reply. Mom would snap her fingers, clap her hands, hug everyone and smile. I can still see her dancing a jig and moving her legs in her enthusiastic state of song.

Even in her distress, Mom would fill another person's heart with happiness. Still, she was slipping away. In spite of everything, Mom and Dad were faithful, loving parents and grandparents every step of the way. We were always together.

And so it was, when Dad, Mom, Dave and I went to the Lahey Hospital and Medical Center, in Burlington, Massachusetts. In his continuous advocacy, Dad had gotten her in for a diagnosis. All four of us drove back and forth for several appointments. Dr. Yuval Zabar, MD, Neurologist, Neurological Surgeon, was her attending doctor. It was on November 9th, 2011, after Dr. Zabar's testing was done that we found out Mom did have Alzheimer's.

I will never forget Mom's elation at not having aphasia. Seriously, she wept over this wonderful news. Mom had spent so much energy on her other illness, only to get worse. She continually forgot that stupid word, 'aphasia' over and over again. Now, she was relieved to know she had Alzheimer's. Mom had progressed so far that it never occurred to her what she actually had… only that she didn't have Primary Progressive Aphasia. Her Mother and her sister died from related complications with this disease. God, in His mercy, spared her from ever understanding that she would, too. Dad also seemed assured. Dr. Zabar would prescribe medication, and see them in a year. "See, it's not that bad…" was my parents' attitude. I was devastated by this news.

My heart dropped to my feet. Something told me that Dr. Zabar knew that I knew, too.

I have decided that there exists, in the medical profession, a collective ability to assess the family dynamics in a nanosecond. I experienced this with the hospice people also. They have a way of seeing which roll each of us has, in a terminal illness. They seem to be able to pick up on it almost immediately.

As we moved into 2012, I knew it was to be a year of lasts… a year of bittersweet goodbyes, and I never stopped crying. I no longer cared if my kids were mad at me, I no longer cared if the church fell apart, I no longer cared about my friends' problems, and I no longer cared about anything but seeing my Mom. My world became a shadow of sadness.

Our last appointment to The Lahey Hospital was on October 30th, 2012. Mom did a good job with her updated testing, according to Dad. She did match words to pictures but when it came time for her reading test, the results weren't nearly as encouraging. She read a full paragraph in what sounded more like "pig latin." Not a single word was accurate but she smiled and looked at "Daddy" and Dr. Zabar, as splendid as a peacock. Dad was so very proud of her. It was for me, a picture to feast one's eyes on. Dad requested yet another follow up, with the fine doctor, in which they were to return in April 2013. Mom never made it. As we left the office patient cubicle, Dad walked up ahead of us to the receptionist. Mom stood waiting, thinking that Dr. Zabar wanted to speak to her. I gently took her arm to direct her out. The last words this daughter heard her Mother shout out, as she waltzed away from this dear man were, "Isn't he just gorgeous!" Yes Mother, he's gorgeous.

Side Note: For my birthday, in December of 2011, and one month after Dr. Zabar's announcement, Mom made me a book of her life. It is very sweet to me, complete with stick people, plain box houses, and single word descriptions. Yet, there were two special entries, close to her heart that she wrote out clearly. One was titled, "Banks of the Susquehanna," the place where she grew up. The second was, "Love of My Life," referring to when she met Dad. For all that, Mom was losing in the battle, she held tightly to both writings, as they were the measure of her mental homesickness.

Knowing You

All I once held dear, built my life upon,

All this world reveres and wars to own.

All I once thought gain I have counted loss,

Spent and worthless now compared to this.

Now my heart's desire is to know You more,

To be found in You, and known as Yours.

To possess by faith what I could not earn,

All surpassing gift of righteousness.

Oh to know the power of Your risen life

And to know You in Your sufferings.

To become like You in Your death, my Lord,

So with You to live and never die.

By Graham Kendrick

Do I like my coffee black? There are other colors?

Just the Facts: It will become too difficult or dangerous for a person with Alzheimer's to be left alone. Preventing wandering becomes a crucial part of care, and safety precautions will need to be taken throughout the person's living environment.

There is something about autumn that calls for a time of reflection. September is when the reality of summer's end hits me and I ask myself how it went by so very fast. Nonetheless, the wonder of fall, the crisp smell in the air combined with the impending cold of winter, create a sense of awe worthy of embracing. It is a season of new beginnings, the start of the school year and the bountiful harvest of potatoes and apples.

For those of us who were changed as a result of September 11th 2001, it is a time to count our blessings. I will never forget that day or the memories that followed.

Our son was 9 years old and playing in a youth football league with Dave as his coach. On their first practice after this terrible event, the boys all "took a knee" and prayed. They were young, and likely didn't understand the full impact of what had happened. No, these boys of fall only really knew that, for the first time in their lives, the adults in their community walked around in an open state of mourning. I'll not forget the first Saturday that followed. How a small neighborhood of families came together on a school field to watch these young ones play some football! I watched as parents, grandparents, uncles, aunts, sisters, brothers and friends walked into the sunlight morning to come together in solidarity; steeled game faces with tear stained determination.

My parents came that day too. The visibility of their pain pierced my soul. I knew the older people were in shock to have witnessed, in their lifetime, this heinous crime against their country. I believe that every able man on that gridiron that particular September day would have gladly taken up arms to defend their homes and country. The bombing of the World Trade Center was personal and the wound was deep. For weeks, even months, people treated one another with decency, graciousness and sympathy.

I recently remarked to my husband that it is one thing, in life, to go through a profound moment. It is quite another thing when a profound moment changes us. Like "the cross," we poise ourselves in boldness to not be shaken, standing firm on the cornerstone of His salvation.

I once again entered into September 2013, reflecting on the past and praying to Almighty God for wisdom, discernment and understanding.

Throughout 2012, I watched, soaked in and took part in as much as I possibly could, of Mom and Dad's life. I had nightmares and unbelievable anxiety, anticipating a phone call any minute. I slept with the phone by my side, never knowing when Mom would take a permanent turn for the worse. It seemed to me that every time I was with her could be the last.

As with holidays for the previous 13 years, Easter was at our house in Portland. I felt certain that my parents would not be able to come and I was fully ready to go to them, but Dad said Mom wanted to drive over. He and I discussed a plan to make dinner quick and easy. They would arrive and we were to eat at noon since Mom got so tired after that. They came, ate, Mom did a couple of dishes, and then they left. It was all of an hour.

Doing dishes was Moms self-proclaimed job. Her dishwashing skills were amusing to all of us, and often shocking to our son who seemed to not understand how we could be so nonchalant about allowing her to "have at it" just for her enjoyment. Nate would tilt his head and eyes towards her while looking at me. I'd give him a casual frown and slightly dismiss his concerns, quietly.

There was a time when her dish rack was orderly… the silverware standing tall, plates side by side, and cups drying upside down. Mom was always systematically organized, but now whatever she did was completely disheveled. Like many with Alzheimer's, this is often a person's last valiant attempt and purpose. This would tend to include dishes not fully cleaned, scattered dinnerware, the use of cold water instead of hot…all fulfilling end of life pleasure. How many days in a lifetime does one stand at the sink running water between their fingers, mulling over the day, the dinner, or a family gathering? The sink is like a sanctuary… a reprieve of sorts. It was her final family task. Mom did the dishes until one day, she announced to Dad she was done. She just couldn't do them anymore.

From May, throughout the summer, we all went back and forth to my parents' house. My youngest brother, George, and I were with Mom for Mother's Day and for her birthday. I took pictures, we visited, had lunch, sat on the porch and drank coffee. My oldest brother, Scott, sent her beautiful flowers from his home in California, announcing he'd come in July for a visit.

I come from a line of coffee drinkers. Dad still ends his day on his porch with a cup of coffee before he gets ready for bed. Mom loved her coffee. She drank it black while Dad and I drink it with sugar and milk. One of the first things Dad did the night we lost Mom was to move her coffee cup so that no one could use it. Their coffee time was always special. It held many memories for Dad. He made Mom her coffee every morning for as long as I can remember. It was toward the very end of her life when she stopped drinking it. I don't know if she knew what she was doing but one day, like the dishes, she was done. No more coffee. I still recall Mom's coffee moments and how she held her cup between her hands like it was a priceless antique. She'd take a sip and slurp it in delight.

Mom's coffee cup was white with a colorful rainbow across it. The first rainbow appeared in the Bible after the flood, along with God's assurance never to flood the earth again. Mom cleaved to the promises of God. Each appearance of a rainbow in the sky was a remembrance, to my mother, of God's vow.

"I have set my rainbow in the clouds, and it will be the sign of the covenant between me and the earth."
Genesis 9:13

This was to be our last Mother's Day and birthday together. We just knew it in our hearts. But who can speak such words? Mom was still somehow able to dress herself at that time, though she wore much of the same clothing over and over again. She wore her bright yellow shirt often and it was on her for both of these May Days.

Mom loved it when you took notice of her appearance. I'd say, "Oh Mom you look so pretty!" She'd then put a hand on one side of her head and another on her hip, like a model. She would then pose and take a bow.

How she maintained her joy was stunning!

Mom looked forward to our company and family time. She would jabber on about all kinds of things. She'd walk into her front room, rustle through her treasures and pull out a long forgotten picture to show us, or a piece of paper that somehow had meaning to her.

Always my mom...

Cradled by the evening traffic in the city woods, I walk seeking yet another path around the darkened bend. Fallen trees obscure the way.
Smiling I hear the sound of the singing nights dawning birds. I ponder the shades of green and brown as dusks' light drizzles through, trees majestic in height, or so it seems. My eyes look up at narrows end, across the field I see buttercups waiting for tomorrows morning's dew.

I remember each flower she ever brought me my mom who delights in them all....yellow, pink, purple and blue.
The flowers of the meadows, first lupines, second buttercups and waiting for her turn not last nor least, Queen Anne's lace will soon be budding too.
Oh the joy of the moment, the sweetness of her love...my heart holds her hand and kisses her as the gentleness of her voice hugs me in the night.

Written for my mom on a lovely late summer eve...

July presented other things for Mom to look forward to. My parents had always enjoyed July 4th, and once again, we made the pilgrimage to Stevens Brooks Elementary School. It was just up the road from them, and an ideal spot to see the fireworks. We brought our chairs, listened to the band, visited with Chris and Jim, their very dear friends, and others. Mom and I walked around so she could see people and, as was my obsessive pattern, I took several pictures. I thought the evening had gone well, but afterward she complained to Dad that people laughed, looked at, and made fun of her. The paranoia part of the disease had kicked in. Not once did anyone treat her anything but kindly. She was, once again, imagining things that were not so.

George's birthday is also in July. He and my nephew, Mat, came to Bridgton for a cookout with us whereupon Dad lit the grill and Mom stood visiting. We all gave George a gift but Mom had, what she felt, was a special one. She had taken a dirty soap dish from her bathroom and crumpled a piece of paper around it, like wrapping paper. Standing outside, near the grill, she proudly handed it to him. He was visibly befuddled. I smiled and quietly told George to, "just go with it." Mom had some words to go along with her gift but none of us could understand what she was saying.

Several times, George and I had to gently hold her as she came dangerously close to burning herself on the grill. It was the beginning of real safety issues and a time to "Mommy proof" any environment she was a part of. Soon to come, was Mom's involuntary, erratic game of hide and seek. I started to receive phone calls from Dad as to her taking things, losing them, and causing daily disturbances. I don't think, for a moment, her behavior was intentional, but it did cause for household problems. She was forever misplacing items and Dad was forever looking for various odds and ends.

Soon after George's birthday, Scott came. It was a quick trip, and he spent all of his time with our parents. Scott, Dave and I were prodding Dad to begin some additional in-house help. We could see the writing on the wall, concerning how Mom might not be able to care for herself much longer. This included the possibility that she wouldn't be able to eat independently. We were reading all that we could about her disease and didn't want Dad to be caught in the middle of a maelstrom with no assistance. I really wanted a nurse or someone to be coming in on a regular basis. Dad was adamant that he wasn't ready but promised that when the time came, he would ask. We did finally get help at the end of January 2013, but as I look back on those days prior to getting the help, I don't know how he did it.

I remember that when Scott left, I was sick for him. I cried, wondering what must have gone through his mind as he said goodbye to his mother, not knowing if he would see her alive again. I tried to put myself in his shoes, wondering how hard it must have been to be so far away in San Diego.

In the meantime, I needed to have knee surgery once again, that August, (I had already had 2 knee surgeries in the past). Dave was gone to sea and I was having excruciating pain. I was almost unable to drive and I was using crutches. What terrible timing. I set up my day of surgery, and had Marikay lined up to pick me up afterward. I hired my son's girlfriend to stay and help me out for 2 days. I was hoping to avoid too much time away from Mom and Dad.

In the past, whenever any of us had a medical procedure, the others all stepped up. My parents had helped during my prior recoveries and they intended to now. I warned my doctor and the nurses of my mom's condition. My parents had me call off Marikay's help. Instead, they picked me up and took me in for the surgery themselves. While in the waiting room, I was called to go in for pre-op. Mom got up too. She wanted to come with me and sit until they took me into the operating room. That lasted all of 3 minutes. We walked out back, whereupon she became completely lost. She walked into the bathroom and immediately back out. She was scared by the shower curtain. She thought the nurse was asking her to get ready and she kept spinning in confused circles. I excused myself for a moment and held Mom's hand. All the while, she was still sporting that big smile of hers as I escorted her back to "Daddy."

After my surgery, Mom and Dad came in beside me in the recovery room. Mom was careful, not to talk or draw any attention to herself. Dad dealt with my doctor's orders and they took me home. They drove back and forth from Bridgton to Portland, checking on me, for days. How they found it in themselves to be so attentive was astonishing to me. My parents were just like that. They were always making sure "their Barbie" was ok.

That September, I started taking more pictures than ever. I would drive to Bridgton, past a farm that gave me comfort. I watched the season's sunlight transition and waved at the tractor drivers, plowing the fields. I looked forward to seeing the cows and sheep, stopping regularly to photograph them. I began to use my photos to make short DVD music videos, about 2-5 minutes long. I would sit for hours at night, editing, improving, and telling our story through this medium. Eventually I splurged from a small Sony "point and shoot" camera to a Nikon 3100. It became my distraction. I have returned to those DVD's and they truly reveal memories of my sorrow.

One day, Mom had a doctor's appointment while I was visiting. I drove behind them over to the office in our Jeep Wrangler. I happen to have had the top down and after her appointment Mom got in with me and Dad drove home in their car. As soon as she got in she looked at me with mischief in her eyes and simply said, "Should we go for an ice cream?" I said, "Exactly what I was thinking, too!" and off we went. Mom loved her ice cream cones. She and Dad were forever talking about the best or worst one, all their lives. I think they spent the better part of their summers together searching high and low for the world's best ice cream cone. Sometimes they'd drive for hours. Honestly, I don't think I know of anyone who loved their ice cream more than my parents did.

It was soon after that, into the fall that Dave and I, once again, took Mom for another ice cream cone. Dad was busy doing something and encouraged us to go. We took Mom over to the local "Gazebo" just a block up the road from them. I knew as soon as we got into our Jeep this was to be our last one together. Mom was, as usual, all excited, as my own heart sank in silent pain while smiling and winking at her as to not reveal the heaviness of my spirit. The air was as crisp in shadows, as the evening was cool. Dave had his IPhone and took a few pictures of us. Those simple phone pictures are now near and dear to me.

"And goodnight to the old lady whispering "hush"
Goodnight stars
Goodnight air
Goodnight noises everywhere"

By Margaret Wise Brown

That October, Dave took me to the Fryeburg Fair to walk through the multitude of barns, photographing all the farmyard animals. We held hands, sat at the food booths, ate far too much, and smiled at memories. In the past, Mom and Dad had been with us but it was not to be this year. The last time they had come, Mom thought a big plastic fake cow was real. She had also walked in front of a huge galloping work horse and had been scared out of her wits. No, this was a season of coming together and moving apart, if only to catch our breath.

Soon after, Dave went back to sea. It was, in some ways, easier for me. I had abandoned, in my thinking, "visiting" with my parents as anything normal and I was attempting to interject myself to be by their sides, deliberately. If I could, I would have moved in with them. I had worked out family leave time at my place of employment and all Dad had to do was say the word. He didn't. Dad was a bedrock. It was not until Mom's last week with us that he let me camp out with them. Sometimes I think he was protecting me, yet I was seeing it all unfold before my eyes. To keep me away from some of what they were going through, only made me more uneasy. I was constantly weighing out how not to upset him, while availing myself to them in a split second if necessary. There was an enormous amount of sensitive gymnastics those last 6 months. It was a highly emotional time, maintaining my relationship with my husband who was 100% supportive, but occasionally in my way. It was a juggling act, keeping the peace as best I could with parents and siblings, while not upsetting our already physically and emotionally fragmented father. Yet, on the front burner was the obvious. We were losing Mom. I knew God was sustaining us. I knew that, like the poem, "Footprints in the Sand," He was carrying us.

Footprints in the Sand (in part)

"Lord, You told me when I decided to follow You, You would walk and talk with me all the way. But I'm aware that during the most troublesome times of my life there is only one set of footprints. I just don't understand why, when I need You most, You leave me."
He whispered, "My precious child, I love you and will never leave you, never, ever, during your trials and testings. When

you saw only one set of footprints, it was then that I carried you."

I knew that, no matter what anyone said by way of, "what I needed" or "what they thought was best for me," He was our sufficiency. Like a flint, He kept my eye on the prize, which was the eventuality of walking our Mother home and into His arms.

Side Note: After the September 11th, 2001, World Trade Center terror, we desired to find a church. We purposely looked at finding a good Bible believing body. Dave left the strongholds of Catholicism and gave his life to Jesus. We fell in love with the church we chose, and became active members. More importantly, we became diligent readers of God's word. My husband and I believed that most of what the New Testament compelled us to do was care for the body of believers. We tried to give as much as we were able, to those in church that were in need. Through our involvement, we began to witness disturbing trends and programs which caused us to question the soundness of our beloved church. We began to dig deeply into His word for answers. These trends included, in part, Rick Warren's Purpose Driven Life, Chuck Colson's Ecumenical ideology, Richard Foster's and Dallas Willard's Spiritual Formation, Youth Specialties and Leadership Networks Influences, Rob Bell, Tony Jones and Brian McLaren's Emergent Church, among others. We contacted other apologists, spoke to Pastors, and met with elders. Both Dave and I researched, and were persistent and vocal in calling out the church to defend itself against such false doctrine which was being espoused by those aforementioned. It was in deep sorrow that we eventually left the church we had come to love, exhausted and hurt. God has been our refuge and He is our fortress.

The church is not a building and worship is not a band standing before us, singing. It is the body of believers in which He is the head. Worship is much bigger than "my feelings." Wherever two or more are gathered, He is there.

The fellowship we had poured ourselves into for all those years was silent in our time of need. I do not say this in anger. I say it only as a point of reference as to how even a good intentioned church body can sometimes appear hypocritical. Abiding in a "community" is not the same as abiding in Him. He alone is our sufficiency. When we come to understand that, it is then that He is able to truly dwell in our hearts through faith.

I would like to thank Jana, Ursula, Caryn and Terry for their prayers and words of encouragement.

I know that you too, have busy lives yet you cared enough to bring my family's needs before the throne of God. Thank you also, Little Anna, for your texts that arrived to my phone when I was having a low moment. I am evermore grateful to all of you.

Sometimes love is marred beyond recognition…It is here where we come to understand that true love has no boundaries.

Written by Georgie Ann's daughter 9 days before she was taken to be with our Lord…

Friendships, Blankets and Conversations...

Just the Facts: Caring for a person with Alzheimer's disease at home is a difficult task and can become overwhelming at times. Each day brings new challenges as the caregiver copes with changing levels of ability and new patterns of behavior. As the disease gets worse, people living with Alzheimer's disease often need more and more care.

One of the determining factors to our parents moving back to Bridgton from Gray, was familiarity. In talking to Dr. Jennifer Smith, Mom's primary hometown doctor, it was suggested that Mom was likely more confused and disorientated because they had moved. It was this that made Dad ultimately decide to return.

It did make a difference for Mom to be in Bridgton. She somehow understood she was, again, near her beloved Stevens Brook Elementary School. She also was more comfortable with going to the grocery store, her hair dressers, and the local pharmacy. The move had proven to offer a positive pattern of harmony.

Mom's hairdresser, Amy, was a woman who at one time, was Mrs. Forney's kindergarten student. She was tender and delicate toward Mom. Not once did Amy let on that Mom wasn't well. Amy conversed and visited with her as though Mom understood everything she talked about. At the local Hannaford grocery store, Mom walked the isles with Dad, saying "hello" to all whose attention she could garner, and then some. Mom treated whomever she saw as though they were a long lost family member.

Mom was blessed to have had several dedicated and loyal friends. She had worked with many over the years, doing Bible studies together and praying with, and for them. When she could no longer go out, they came to her. When she could no longer remember their names, they remembered hers.

A friend is someone who knows the song in your heart and can sing it back to you when you have forgotten the words.

Albert Camus

Her friends would sing to her, hold her hand and sit and read the Bible to her. Some brought meals, homemade bread and flowers. Martha her ardent, enthusiastic and devoted friend, would take Mom in her arms, and dance. She showered Mom with hugs, singing children's nursery rhymes and Bible songs all the way up until the very end of Mom's life. One of the last things Mom said to Martha was, "You're on your own now."

Thank you Martha, Gayle, Chris, Linda, Joanne, Jan and the many others for your tried and true friendship toward Georgie

Mom talked often about going out with her friends. She really wanted to. In her mind, I think she thought she was. To hear her talk, she was heading to the school for a visit, sitting at the lake for a picnic lunch, or getting picked up to go for breakfast. In the late fall of 2012, Mom thought she was going to a party where there'd be dancing. I can't remember exactly what it was she assumed she was doing but she was very excited. For about 2 weeks, every time I saw her, she'd dance, curtsy, and laugh, getting a kick out of her own festivity.

All of her girlfriend flashbacks played in her head as though they were current events. She'd smile and tell me stories over and over again. Mom would be talking, then sort of shake her head and look at me as though she hadn't known I was there, as though I'd caught her by surprise.

I'd be sitting beside her on the couch where she'd be all wrapped up in her blanket. Mom would gaze out to nowhere, or somewhere. Only she knew. She'd say her friends' names out of context and her mind seemed to wander off to a place in the past, or in mid-sentence, forget a whole thought. Mom might sit quietly for a moment then exclaim, "Now I remember!" and then go off on an entirely new incongruent story. I paid close attention to her words, attempting to catch a clear one now and then, so that I might encourage her. I really wanted to understand what she was saying. I didn't want to miss anything Mom was able to share with me, Alzheimer's or not. It was all so important. I always had a sense that she needed someone to cherish and keep forever, every important facet of her life and all she cared about.

"Let's take a nap," she'd say, and then lie down on the couch. I'd tuck her in, sit at her feet, look at her and smile. She'd wave at me, smiling back as her eyes closed slowly, as she was assured I was not leaving. Mom would rest for a while, wake up, and start all over again.

Sometimes, she'd sit upright and sleep in my arms, on my shoulder, head to head, or sometimes we'd go to her bed and climb in. I say "climb in," because that was a chore in itself. Mom and Dad's bed was the high kind. My parents should have probably had a hospital bed but they wanted to remain in theirs, if possible. Yet, there existed a very real problem in getting Mom into this "princess and the pea" bunk. Dad was the only one who could successfully do this. He had a system. Mom could no longer distinguish how to move her little body parts to get into their bed and for 120 pounds, she was all dead weight. She couldn't understand how to step up on a footstool, or how to lift her legs. Once, when I was attempting to help her, she pushed me out of the way. While standing in place, she ran as fast as her legs would run, jumped up about one half of an inch and landed in the same place beside her bed. It was all I could do to contain myself from belly laughing aloud or falling to the floor sobbing. Take your pick. In all of 30 seconds I was in dually competing emotions. She was brilliant and like the upside down book reading, she was my astounding Mother, who never ceased to amaze me.

Our son, Nate, eventually went to Grammy's and Grampy's house to cut their bed down. He and Dad measured and sawed the legs so that Mom could more easily sit on the side and then lay down.

As I think back to many of those days, I wish I could have adequately portrayed the picture in my mind's eye on paper. There were times when Mom was like a baby, babbling words that were nonsensical to anyone but herself. I was a parent, patiently listening to a child's utters and murmurs. She would blurt out full, unrecognizable sentences. Mom would raise her head off of her pillow, look at me wide eyed as though she knew I was grasping what she was saying but it was not the case. It seemed to me she was telling me her whole life story, her voice inflecting emotion, or her face frowning inquisitively. Mom was not a quiet Alzheimer's victim. She chatted gibberish until the very end, with her hands held together like "the church and the steeple" and her precious blanket in-between them, while her thumbs were in constant motion.

I am not sure how this dear old red blanket became "hers." Mom would wrap herself up in it. Sometimes she'd have it draped across her shoulders or over her legs. She played with it, folding and re-folding it and pulling at the fringes, making an ironed looking pattern over her arm, obsessively rubbing it smooth. Toward the end, she abandoned her meticulousness and began to just roll it up in a ball. Like her books, purse, and Bakelite jewelry, it became another one of "her favorite things." This, along with a special sweater and beat up pair of grey slippers, were like a young one's pleasure to her. They hardly ever left her side during her last months. Dad was continuously washing the blanket and sweater and putting her slippers near her whenever she moved. We attempted to have her wear pretty new ones that Nate had bought his grandmother, but she would have none of that. They hurt her feet, though we exchanged them twice for larger ones.

Dad found out that it is true, about Alzheimer's patients wearing the same clothes over and over again. He admirably kept up and constantly found ways to adjust. When Mom was insisting her clothes were clean and she'd want to re-wear them, Dad began to quietly hide them in the laundry basket where she had, by then, forgotten to look. He started to lay out her clothes, coaxing her toward another wardrobe choice. Dad also began to go through her bureau drawers, discreetly removing her clothing and consolidating choices for her. Quickly, as this phase of laying out clothes ended, he jumped in to help her dress. Little by little, Mom wasn't able to care for herself. It began with simple things like putting her arm in a shirt or pulling up her pants.

Sometimes Dad would get her dressed, only to walk away and find her altogether undressed a short time later! Yes, I do mean undressed completely. For anyone who has worked with and cared for a person with a disease of the mind, this happens to be one moment that is feared more than just about any other. Rest assured, it will happen, and likely more than once. It is during that very sensitive time when we all want to uphold the dignity of those we love.

For us, this was the point when "dignity" left on the last train out of Dodge. On more than one occasion, I received a close to hysterical phone call from my modest father concerning his once modest wife.

Side Note: Aqua is my favorite color. It reminds me of the ocean in the Dominican Republic where Dave and I have gone to vacation. Dave is at sea 6 months out of the year, and we indulge ourselves yearly in a getaway of heat, books quiet and beach walks. We enjoy this time of no interruptions and one to one conversation. Because of Mom's illness, our "retreat" time the past few years has gone from 7 days, to 6 days to 5 days… and even then, I got very fidgety. It is the color I landed on when I decided to crochet a blanket the last year Mom was with us.

Mom loved to crochet, and my Aunt Donnie did needlepoint. Over the years, they both made me lovely Christmas ornaments in their preferred crafts. Mom made me several little snowflakes, while Donnie did small square ones with words.

I only ever crocheted my blanket while I was with Mom and it was made with one of her crochet hooks. I brought it every time I came to see her, in a basket she had given me. Crocheting was familiar to Mom and doing this project with just the two of us was a way of bringing us both comfort. When I first began this project, Mom would hold the yarn and twist it as though she were helping me. She'd just reach out to feel the softness with her fingers. Eventually, she would just look at it and tell me how pretty it was. Toward the end of Mom's days with us, she no longer noticed what I was doing, yet I continued beside her… yarn in my hands and basket at our feet.

On the day we lost Mom, my brother George and I were sitting beside her bed quietly, visiting as Mom lay in a coma. He asked about our blanket and I told him how it symbolized mine and Mom's personal time together. As we sat there, I finished the blanket and announced to Mom that it was finally done and that it was very pretty. Poor George said to me "That's it? You have nothing more to do?"

"Nope" I said, "We're all done."

After we lost her, I was showing the blanket to our daughters. As I held it up I had a good chuckle. Apparently, I had lost count of the rows. My aqua colored crochet was actually a splendid triangle. Yana suggested I unravel the yarn and fix it. How could I? It was perfect. It holds all those days weaved together, in stored up memories.

The Last Supper and Christmas

Just the facts: As with physical symptoms, every patient's emotional needs in the final stages of life also differ. However, some emotions are common to many patients during end-of-life care. Many worry about loss of control and loss of dignity as their physical abilities decline. It's also common for patients to fear being a burden to their loved ones. Yet, at the same time, they also fear abandonment.

By November, 2012, Mom had begun to show signs of physical deterioration. She was experiencing more and more difficulties eating and she was plagued with UTI, or urinary tract infections.

The UTI affected her mental stability and she was no longer able to communicate her problems, so it became harder for Dad to know when something was wrong with her. She had these infections in the past, but as Mom began to get weaker they were beginning to come in shorter frequency. Mom would become more erratic than usual and Dad would begin the process of figuring out what was amiss for her. Alzheimer's patients often die of complicated illnesses related to it. Late stage Alzheimer's prevents a person's ability to communicate their physical "hurts," leaving caregivers with many real concerns. It is often a guessing game and the very nature of this problem causes the stress level to go up.

Dad was constantly adjusting to Mom's mental decline, but now her physical functions were starting to slowly fall apart too. It was often hard to tell which was mental and which was a physical medical dilemma, needing to be addressed. I became more and more alarmed, knowing that this type of reoccurring infection could lead to Mom's death. There is an immense amount of "sifting through the fog" for caregivers at end of life, especially when the illness is so complex and has many facets to keep up with. It is no wonder a caregiver can be at "wits end" on a regular basis. To his credit, Dad kept himself pulled together more than could ever have been expected. He was determined to take care of his wife.

He was also in charge of the kitchen and of Mom's ever changing food desires. "Ever changing" is probably not an adequate way to describe what was happening with Mom's eating habits. Truth be told, she was losing the capacity to eat or to distinguish what she was eating. Dad was always providing food, drinks, and treats for her. He thought of nothing else but, "what would she like." He'd ask her and she'd tell him, but once a meal was made and in front of her, she began to question it. She would, at times, ignore her plate and pick up a paper napkin roll it up and, if he hadn't been sitting there, she would have eaten that instead. She started to put things on her food and then she'd announce to Dad, "I've always eaten it like this," which of course, she had not.

Dad bought Mom her childhood favorite "Lebanon bologna." She preferred to eat her sandwiches on plain white burger rolls. Mom and Dad were originally from Lock Haven, Pennsylvania, and for anyone who knows anything about that culture, this luncheon meat is a pure love! Mom always said:

"The only sandwich there ever was, was sweet Lebanon Bologna."

She also loved birch beer soda and Dad made sure it was always in the refrigerator. He did all he could to be sure she ate healthy, but in the end he abandoned those worries, exchanging them for, "I just want her to eat something… anything." It's just like us to feel that if only a person would eat, then all would be well. Eating seems to be the gauge we all hold onto. Eating and drinking are the indicators that tell us the body is breaking down. It is literally a barometer telling us that end of life may be beginning. The body gets ready, reserving internal strength for the journey. In our desperately helpless way, we cannot fathom this as being a natural and normal process. Dad did all he could to be sure Mom ate. He tried to convince me she was eating enough. I knew he thought she was, but she was beginning to eat for end of life and that was actually very little.

Death is a mystery…the months, weeks and days leading up to it are hard to understand. Who, in their right mind, is looking at their loved one and saying, "the journey has begun." We know it in our panicked minds as we witness their days and adjust to their needs, but to discern the signs seems unfathomable. Like any terminal illness that lingers in a long "good-bye," we were both blessed and pained at what we witnessed happening to our dear one.

Mom's health rallied for Thanksgiving 2012, which in many ways, was like her last "supper." I made a big meal at my house, preparing the whole dinner in a large pan. I made turkey, potatoes (white and sweet), stuffing and vegetables; all in a convenient "pop into the oven" fashion. I made the pies, bread and cranberry sauce, then packed it all up. My son and I then hopped into the Jeep and set out for Bridgton. Dad set up dishes and drinks, and my brother George, drove from New Hampshire to join us. There were only the five of us since we felt that we needed to keep this day soft hearted and gentle.

What a time Mom had! She thoroughly relished the meal. Our Mother smiled and ate, then ate, and smiled some more. She mistook who Nate and George were, as she sat across the table from them, but she just smiled, ate even more, and kept turning her head towards "Daddy" with a brilliant twinkle in her eyes. Mom's joy on that day was contagious. All the food in that pan was put together in small "Mommy" pieces. She could just spoon it up and have her fill…. and she did.

Dave had been gone for Thanksgiving, but returned in December. Dad had some business in Connecticut and asked if Dave would drive with him while I babysat Mom. Dad thought it best that Mom come to our house, so he brought her on two early mornings that they went to Connecticut. The last time Mom had been to my house, I had driven her in our Jeep from Bridgton. As we drove down our rode, she said to me, "Who lives on this road?" I replied, "I do." She then said to me "I didn't know that." Nevertheless, we knew she was familiar with our house from all the years she'd been coming and it would give her a pleasant and safe break from their home.

After all, we were heading into Christmas and she and I could do things together. The first day she came, I set up my dining room with ornaments and wreath making accessories. I had already put the tree up and I made sure the lights were on as well. I even set a fire in the fireplace. Mom and I took naps together. I had snacks prepared, but Mom wasn't able to do much. When I fed her, she was at a loss as to how to eat. She'd take her straw and try to suck up her yogurt, or take her spoon to eat her orange juice. Her fingers were hastily becoming her utensil of choice. She enjoyed the quiet music in the background, but she had no idea what I was doing with the wreaths. After resting on the couch where I could smile and wave at her from our dining room project, Mom would get up. She would come to the table briefly, but did not touch anything, or take any interest in what I was doing. Unlike our days in the past, Mom and I didn't "God talk," since she wasn't coherent enough. I did, at one time, bow my head to pray with her but even this gesture of bonding made her agitated, so I stopped almost immediately, my spirit heavy within.

The second day Mom came, I pre made cookie dough, hoping this would be a pleasure for her but like the time before, she wasn't aware of much.

That day, I took Mom into the bathroom. I drew a nice bath, grabbed a warm snuggly robe and towels to cover her. I had stepped into a new phase of caregiving.

God alone, knows the days of our life. He knew I would become a mother like daughter, to a childlike mother.

I was also able to help Mom simply write, "Mom," on two Christmas cards. Our card was homemade, with a picture of one of her crocheted snowflakes hanging in our tree with a Bible verse. To the best of my knowledge, these were her last written words. It took much effort, but she did write her name. We gave the cards as "gifts," to her sons, Scott and George.

One of the things that was distinctly different this day with Mom was how she didn't obsess over "Daddy" coming back. In the past, when she and I were alone, she would stand by the window looking for him to return. Whether in Bridgton or in Portland, she'd walk to the window and say to me, "Don't you think he's been gone a long time?" Now she was beginning to forget the most important person in her world. I had grown used to her fretfulness about being apart from him, if only for an hour. Mom's eyes followed Dad at all times. She had to see him and know where he was, always. She became completely dependent on him. To be with her and witness yet another example of her mental decline shook me up.

For Christmas, my brother Scott, and nephew, Zach, made a trip home to visit. Our daughter Tracy, her husband Roger, our son Nate, Dave, and I were all planning on a visit to Grammys and Grampys, too. By this time, I knew that too many people would cause confusion for Mom but as her days were becoming obviously short, all who were able, needed to come together one last time for her and Dad.

Our parents live in a small house, and to have nine people together did cause a great deal of commotion. Mom was visibly disorientated. There was conversation, joking, gifts, and take-out Chinese food. Dad, Scott and Dave did the guy shuffle…. "I'm paying for it,"… "No, I'm paying!" The boys teased Dad and gave him a hard time…because they could… and he laughed. Scott and Dave had become friends over the years and I was grateful that they had one another and that together, they were doing their best to see Dad through in "guy speak."

Poor Mom looked at everyone, unable to really engage. The talking and noise made her very tired. Dad and I put her into bed several times but true to Mom's love of family, she kept getting up to join the "party." I watched her closely, her eyes now becoming devoid of all understanding. Her beautiful smile had become pasted in place with no verbal response. She was quiet. She did not comprehend any of the gifts and she ate very little.

As the day progressed, we were in a way, coming to the stark reality that this was it. Lights out. Our dear mother was leaving us.

This day was my final picture of Mom. I was unable to photograph her afterward… seeing how her enchanting sweet face had left us. It was my moment of truth and from that day forward, I needed to remember my Mom as she once was, not like how she was becoming in her last days on this earth. I turned off my camera to any further pictures of her. What I couldn't turn off was what was to come, nor my deep love of both of my parents, along with my commitment to see them through until the very end.

As we headed into January, 2013, Mom's condition took a turn for the worse. There began to be more physical signs that her body was rapidly breaking down. Her urinary tract infection reappeared and was not going away for any significant amount of time. She was going through all the antibiotics available to her. Additionally, her ability to swallow medicine was becoming an issue. Mom's skin was drying out, showing symptoms of dehydration. Dad bought every skin cream under the sun, rubbing it on her back and body to bring relieve. He gave her as much fluid as she would drink, constantly bringing a glass full of liquid to her.

Dad hadn't yet lined up additional help for them, and we could see the writing on the walls, which were swiftly closing in. It was all happening so fast that hardly a day went by when he was able to catch his breath, let alone consider what he needed to help them get by. This had been a very real concern for my brother Scott, Dave, and myself in July of 2012, but now it was here. Mom's all out uncontrollable attack of her Alzheimer's began January 6th, 2013.

Side Note: Over the years of my parents' marriage, somewhere along the way, they no longer had their wedding rings. Mom still had her diamond but not the band. Dad, I believe, had lost his ring. When they had been married 50 years, they both renewed their love for one another and bought new shiny gold bands. With Mom's disease, she had problems with her rings so she took them off daily, before bedtime. Every morning, Dad would get her rings, put them back on her finger and give her a kiss, telling her he loved her.

No one can say what is right or what is wrong when it comes to end of life decisions. They present some of the hardest choices a person is faced with. Living wills or a person's wishes must be honored. Comfort, pain management, dignity and medical treatment is a family's duty to uphold. Seeing death and dying through until the end, is the most difficult privilege anyone can be expected to endure.

I don't know how people say goodbye permanently. The Bible talks about peace… "a peace that passes all understanding"…. in Philippians, chapter 4, only after Paul exhorts the believers to "stand strong in the Lord."

While my mom was going through her days of Alzheimer's, I did not experience peace as a feeling, but rather, peace as truth and knowledge that "He who began a good work in us" would see us through until the end. My peace is, "The God of Peace". Far too often, my brothers and sisters in Christ put the emphasis on something other than God. They chase after a feeling, instead of chasing after the Almighty.

Be still, and know that I am God;
I will be exalted among the nations,
I will be exalted in the earth!
Psalms 46:10

"Be still" is one thing, but knowing that "He is God" makes all the difference. If I were to place my trust in anything but Him, I would be sorely disappointed. To trust even my feelings, is not to trust in Him.

Dad stood strong in spite of everything turning against them. In his frenzied days in the last 3 months, he wondered out loud as to whether he was doing the "right" thing by Mom. He thought that maybe…. just maybe …. he should put her into a home/hospital. I knew that whatever he was feeling, he would regret that decision for the rest of his days. Fortunately, his fears were short lived and he remembered his pact with Mom to keep her home with him.

Mom's own mother was put into a facility where her Alzheimer's psychosis caused the staff to be so concerned that they took away her bed and left her with only a mattress on the floor.

No, Dad would take no chances. That would not be the fate of his beloved wife.

Months turn into weeks, turn into days...

Just the Facts: The experience of dying is different for each person. It comes in its own time and its own way. However, the process of dying often follows a somewhat predictable path. Several physiological changes signal that death is near. Knowing what to expect during this difficult time can alleviate some of the fears and worries. When a person with Alzheimer's disease is in the very late stages of the disease, the focus should be on quality of life and comfort, rather than on lengthening life and administering treatment.

What was to come as the end of life drew near for Mom was, in some ways, shocking. Never did we expect our dear Mother, who had been nothing but good, kind, and full of abundant love, to become so helpless and out of control. I can somewhat understand how people abandon a loved one with Alzheimer's, preferring instead, to remember them the way they had been and not the way they become from this horrible illness of the mind.

As I witnessed this transition in the last 2 ½ months of Mom's life, I knew it was "time." As the days became painfully difficult, Dad began to solicit my advice regarding everything. Whenever he needed help or council he would say, "We are doing this together." Not a single choice involving Mom's welfare was decided without the two of us in agreement. Yet, there were agonizing decisions that had to be made. Often, without any time to actually process what was happening to her. She deteriorated so fast that as I look back today, I know it was only by God's strength that Dad ever got through it.

Dad called me on January 6th, 2013. This day marks the beginning of the end, the start of his wife fully leaving him mentally. From this day forward, Mom barely understood anything. Her mind left her as her body broke down. She was having no control over her actions.

There is no other way to describe Mom's behavior other than frenzied. I went back and forth from our house, constantly. Dad continued to call me with details of yet another challenging day or night. Unlike our understanding of end of life Alzheimer's victims being lethargic and often unable to move around, Mom never slept. She would doze and nap, but she hardly went to bed for any length of time, staying up all night. She didn't sleep much during the day, and she was anything but docile.

Mom would get up and roam the night away, rolling up scatter rugs, putting them in corners, emptying out drawers, moving books from the shelves, and opening and closing doors. Dad was unable to stop her and resolved himself to sitting or lying on the couch where he could watch and make sure she was safe and not hurting herself. He did this night after long night. As was his way, Dad wouldn't let anyone relieve him of his duties. I would go during the day to give him a break but he used his freed up time to go get groceries, do laundry, run to the dump or go to the post office. It made Dad uneasy to leave Mom. Though many offered to stay with her, he was nervous to be away, if only for an hour. There was no convincing him of going off to "take time for himself." It was not until 3 weeks before Mom left us that Dad agreed to have a lady recommended by Hospice, come and "Mommy-sit." That was only twice. By this time, he was fully assisting her in dressing, showering and primping her hair. When it was time to brush her teeth he would stand beside her and show her how as he brushed his own.

People may think they know what's best for us, but in the end, we ultimately do what "we need to do" our way.

As January progressed and Mom continued to digress, we were finally able to convince Dad to see their doctor to get suggestions on help. I was hoping that Dad would ask for hospice since he was now using that word. "Hospice" was a word that did not roll off of my father's tongue with ease. On Friday, January 24th, 2013, we saw Dr. Jennifer Smith. I have been to the doctors with Mom before. She was always engaging and smiling, but on this day she sat quietly and barely moved while Dad and I talked. Dad did ask for help but he minimized their need, never using that scary word, "hospice". All I can say is "Thank-you Dr. Jennifer!" She saw right through all of it, having cared for and been such a loving medical professional to Mom for many years. The very next day, Dad got a phone call and in two days a nurse was at their house. I was still a bit apprehensive, but I was impressed with how quickly a small town doctor's office was in taking care of "its own." I am grateful, not only for this, but for what was to come with Androscoggin County Hospice.

By Monday, Mom and Dad had an assigned nurse who would come a few times a week and who was only a phone call away. As Dave and I left Bridgton from a visit, all seemed ok. While driving back to Portland, I got online to see if a particular hotel in New York City had openings. At the last minute we decided to take a quick bus trip. We caught a bus that very evening and booked a two day pass for the "Hop-on Hop-off" city tour in the Big Apple. I packed my camera and off we went. We spent all

of our time riding on top of a double decker bus while Dave patiently let me click away to the music of the camera. We saw sights we hadn't seen before and made our yearly pilgrimage to the World Trade Center Memorial. As we were heading back from our 48 hours away, I talked to Dad, only to find out that Mom had become more erratic… as if that was possible.

The following week, even with a home care nurse checking on Mom, she got worse. Between the nurse and her doctor, some medicine adjustments were made with the hope of calming her down. Mom's Alzheimer's fought harder and she continued to go without sleep. All the while she was in an accelerated state of business. Both my parents were still going without sleep and Mom was maintaining her pattern of raising total havoc in their house.

Dave headed back to work on the west coast on February 5th. As with my brother Scott, having to leave his mother often to go back west, I was stricken with deep sadness now, for my husband. I watched as he said goodbye to "Bob and Georgie" knowing full well what was before them. It was time for him to go back to work which meant 2 months away, and he knew that this was his "goodbye" to a woman he had come to love and cherish. As he enveloped her into his arms for what he knew was his final good bye, he longingly hugged her, paused, and then gently kissed her cheek. Dave was visibly heartbroken and couldn't even speak as we got in the car and drove away. Dad held Mom beside him as she blew kisses at Dave, smiling and waving goodbye. She was the most beautiful person in the world, at that moment.

On February 7th, Dad and I sat with their nurse and asked about hospice care. We had both spoken prior to her arrival and were in agreement about the questions we were now ready to address. This was one of the hardest days of my life. This was the day we came face to face with stark reality. Mom was dying and now we needed to ask the very hard questions on how to proceed in the most honorable way. It was the way that we understood what Mom would have wanted. Together, with the nurse, we decided to stop administering her Alzheimer's medicine. We began to fully treat her psychotic symptoms and see if we could give her some peace. Mom was suffering beyond what was even close to mental reasonability, and well past what was normal for surviving Alzheimer's victims.

Androscoggin County Hospice arrived and did an interview on February 12th. by the 14th, she was under their palliative care. We came up with a plan and goal. The plan was to try to get control over her daily behavior so she might get some rest and to keep her home to die in her own bed. The first was never successful but the second was accomplished.

Mom never stopped until the day she landed in a semi-coma. Eventually, she slipped into full a coma 7 to 8 days before we lost her.

Dad and I took over for most of her care, having the hospice nurses come check in, make recommendations, medicine adjustments, take Mom's vitals, and help us keep our heads on. They helped when needed, with the incontinence, since Mom's was quite extreme. They ordered and delivered equipment which was meant to help with bathing, along with other bathroom activities. They were available 24/7 by phone. Mom got so bad that there was even talk of putting her temporarily into the hospital, but after some thought we mutually agreed that the goal of her dying at home could be at risk. Dad was completely attentive to Mom and she was never in any danger. The other concern was that, to move Mom would have been devastating for her, causing her to fully go over the edge. No, she needed to stay put.

As for us, we needed divine, supernatural strength to walk her home to Jesus.

The last weeks were filled with riddles and very few answers. I don't think Mom knew who I was most of the time. One day, while I was helping her dress, she resisted me as I was trying to put her right arm in her right sleeve. She kept trying to put it in the left sleeve. Mom simply looked at me, pointing a finger, and said, "I hope the next lady is nicer." She utterly made me laugh inside. "Good, Mom, I hear words and they are beautiful,…" is what I thought. Another time, while aiding her in the bathroom, all of a sudden she affectionately said, "Oh Barbara…" again, words. All I longed for was to hear her talk. By this time, she was mostly walking to the window and sitting on a stool, making jesters and noises, then getting up and walking to another place and repeating her banter to a different wall, door, chair or window. Mom did some things that there are no words for. To this day, Dad and I are working to erase them from our thoughts. It is a sad illness, yet the oxymoron is that I am so thankful to have been a part of all of it with them. For something so beyond our control, I wouldn't change the importance of walking through this, united in devotion. When it's all said and done, there should be no regrets where love has been.

Side Note: Mom was estranged from her younger daughter for many years. Dad kept my sister Suzanne, who lives in Florida, informed concerning our Mother. There were many things that my parents felt bad about regarding this relationship. It is hard to put distance between yourself and a child who for whatever reason, has chosen to live a life of "victimhood." Over the years, my sister has taken advantage of others, using them for money most of her adult life. Since the 80's she has also been a member of a cult. Dad was disturbed that Sue never called Mom or asked about her in any of their conversations. It was a strain which I was sensitive to, during Mom's last weeks with us. Paying for, and inviting her home was not an option with all that he was facing.

On the last day that Mom was with us, I was asked to talk to her to her about any unresolved issues she might have. This was the one I talked to Mom about as she lay in a coma. I prayed over her and talked to her about Suzanne. I've no doubt Mom loved her but there are some things this side of heaven we cannot know or understand, even when they are as close and personal as this was. I assured her it was ok and that, "God's got this one too, Mom."

Our brother Scott has checked in and helped Sue and her children over the years. He did reach her and offered to bring her to Maine for Mom's memorial. Sue did come. Soon after, she left. It has now been several months since Dad has heard from her.

Trumpet Call...

Just the Facts: Often before death, people will lapse into a coma. A coma is a deep state of unconsciousness in which a person cannot be aroused. Persons in a coma may still hear what is said even when they are no longer able to respond. They may also feel something that could cause pain, but not respond outwardly. Caregivers, family, and physicians should always act as if the dying person is aware of what is going on and is able to hear and understand voices. In fact, hearing is one of the last senses to lapse before death.

Three days before Mom went into a semi-coma, I sat reading to her on their couch. Dad had run off to the grocery store to pick up a few things. Deborah, Mom's primary hospice nurse, had just taken Mom's vitals and was in the dining room entering the information into her computer. It was a cold winter's eve as I pulled 2 books from Mom's bookshelf to sit with her.

Mom was wrapped in her blanket as I moved in close to her with her Bible, and Dr. Seuss' Oh the Places You'll Go. (The second book was given to her by Stevens Brook School when she retired. It had all her teacher friends and family member names signed in it). I opened one book and then the other. Mom's hands stayed in place as I reached out and delicately took one in my own. With our hands held together, I slowly turned a page or two, reading aloud. I extended one of Mom's fingers to feel the paper as we flipped the pages. I could barely read the words. My voiced cracked as I witnessed my Mother letting go of her dearly beloved books.

When Deborah was finished, she silently got up from her work, looked me in the eye with that ever knowing hospice nurse face, and left without saying a word. She was leaving a mother and a daughter alone in this sensitive moment.

It was the last time I ever sat on the couch with my Mom.

Dad called me on Monday night, March 18th, to say Mom had gone to bed but she hadn't moved, and he was very worried. It had begun to snow and a storm was predicted for that night and into Tuesday. When I talked to Dad Tuesday morning, Mom had still not moved. Dad wanted me to stay put because he didn't want me driving in the snow, which by now was coming down strongly. I waited all day in Portland, talking to him frequently. Because of the weather the hospice nurse had not been to their house, either. I started to occupy myself with cleaning our home and packing my bags for Bridgton. On Wednesday morning bright and early, our son carried a camping bed and my overnight bags to the Jeep. I hugged him and told him I didn't know when I'd be back, then drove up to Bridgton. When I arrived, I couldn't get out of the truck quick enough. Mom hadn't moved since Monday evening and Dad had been all by himself, literally standing watch during the storm.

As I entered my parents' bedroom and was leaning over her, Mom opened her eyes and, looking up to me, she mouthed, "You're beautiful." I returned the compliment of love, then held and kissed her.

I had called my brothers on my way up to Bridgton and, as I quickly surmised the situation, I called them again. Coincidentally, Dave was shoreside and I was able to leave him a voice message which I knew he would hear, and return my call as soon as possible.

I don't recall much about that afternoon and evening as the shock sank in. I kept expecting Mom to fully wake up and get out of bed. Dad was attempting to feed her liquids, but she had little response. Mom's mouth hardly moved. Her body was already stiff with her arms and hands in place. One, along her side and one, bent beside her face. She was a portrait, in many ways… pretty and sweet.

As Wednesday evening set in, George called to say he and his ex-wife Sandy would be over on Thursday. Scott, who was in Washington DC at the time, texted to say he was leaving and flying home. Scott's fiancé Elizabeth would be flying in from San Diego, and together they would be also here on Thursday. Dave called and said his boss had given him permission to come home and that he'd be here Friday morning. I know I talked to our children, but it was all a blur. As night came, I opened my "camping cot" in my parent's front room and settled in with an attentive ear for any movement coming from Mom and Dad's bedroom. I was on edge and couldn't sleep.

Around 4 AM, I heard Dad get up. As I looked into the dining room from my cot, I saw him fussing with things that I couldn't quite make out. I called to Dad, asking him what he was doing. He seemed preoccupied so I got up and went to him. Mom had been so at peace that it never occurred to either of us that her body was still working, and she had had an accident. Together, Dad and I began what was to be our last walk together, attending to all of Mom's personal care. Gently working around Mom, we cleaned her bedding, moved her frail body, washed and dried her… together we affectionately whispered words to her to uphold her dignity.

That night was a night of dual concern for me since, shortly after Dad and I were awake, I heard a loud bang in the kitchen. Dad, who had been so consumed with Mom, had neglected his own health. (He has type 2 diabetes and high blood pressure). Dad had taken a fall and was lying on the kitchen floor. I ran to him, forcing back the hysteria as I reached for him on the floor.

"Dad…can you move? Dad…? Dad, I'm going to call an ambulance."

"No, Barbie please don't," he responded.

"Dad…?"

"Please don't, Barbie, I'll be ok."

My parent's kitchen is right beside their bedroom and there he was, barely 10 feet away from his wife. I knew from his hushed words, he didn't want to leave her. He didn't want the ambulance to come and disrupt their home. I knew it would upset him terribly, yet here was my father, flat out on the kitchen floor while Mom lay still in their bed.

"What tragic poetry," my mind said to myself, "I am all alone with my parents. They are going to die right now, and I can't hold them both at the same time…OH my God!"

Dad slowly began to move, and eventually got up.

On Thursday morning, March 21st, I stood staring at the small packet in the palm of my hand. It was a 3 by 1 ½ inch packet with green, red, blue, and white markings. It was balm, given to me by Deborah for administering to Mom's dry lips. In bold letters was the word, "Dyna Lube." In small letters at the bottom left, I read the words "Made in Israel." I stood in my parent's dining room, crying, as Dad and Deborah stared at me. "Read this, Dad," I said, handing him the packet. He too, began to cry.

If ever there was a sign that God was present, it was in this moment. As Mom was in a semi-coma just beside us in the bedroom, I was concerned about her mouth drying out. Deborah had just returned from her car and handed me a handful of these Israeli made packets of lip balm. Tender Israeli lip balm to place on my Mom's lips during her last days with us. Deborah said she had no idea it was made in Israel until now. It was like God's silent end of life secret, revealed.

I am with you always

God

Our family vigil had begun…

When Scott arrived that Thursday, Mom almost got out of bed in a momentary state of lucidity. She said, "I have to get up," and she almost did. She was so overwhelmed with happiness that he was here. We both cradled her, Scott on one side, I on the other, until she fell back into her coma sleep .This lasted all of 60 seconds, yet it was so typical of her to be excited when he came to visit.

The hospice nurses came daily to check on Mom's vitals and to give us feedback about what was happening. We all stood around, anxious for "an answer." Dad and I took over, immediately administering Mom's end of life medicine directives. Mom never seemed to be in pain but we all had discussions and watched the clock concerning how much and how often she should receive medicine. I know that between Dad, Dave, Scott, and I, we were secretly going to our computers searching all we could about end of life and what to expect. It was, I suppose, a way to feel in control of something completely out of our control. Our minds wanted to comprehend the incomprehensible.

By Saturday, Scott and Dave settled themselves into writing an obituary. We bought sandwich meat, bread, cheese, take-out pizza and coffee. Elizabeth helped with laundry and cleaning. We visited, laughed in quiet voices and drank a lot of coffee. At one time, I raised my voice towards Scott ready to have a fight. He simply said to me, "Stop it... Mom's in the next room!" and it was over. I stepped outside often, calling our daughters and our son, and to text Marikay.

We all walked constantly in and out of the bedroom checking on Mom, taking separate time to talk to her, cry over her, and touch her. I kept thinking how sad it was for Mom to not have her own Mother with her. During the end, many of us are orphans, having lost parents already in the past. I kept thinking how much I'd miss having her when my time came and how much I'd miss her for all the little things that only a Mother can provide.

There were extraordinary moments revealed as she headed closer to the tangible presence of God. Mom had 2 profound glimpses into her tomorrows at different times. Once, while I was sitting with her, she raised her arm towards heaven pointing and said, "There's Donna Rae!" The second time, she lifted her hand over her heart and said the words, "My Mother." Both times her face became radiant and angelic. Dad also had a divine minute when once, as he kissed her, his wife opened her eyes clearly and looked right into his own. Oh, Sweet Georgie Ann, a wife and a mother ... was leaving us and heading toward a place we could "only imagine," as invisible angels appeared to be drawing her closer.

Our parents have a cat named "Poogie," who is 23 years old. She has been with them longer than, as Dad says, "You kids ever were." Their cat has got to be the most vicious animal anyone has ever loved. She is protective, possessive and spoiled. She routinely and intentionally circles around "company," looking for a surprise strike, which usually involved a quick paw to the shin, (with claws in….no blood was ever drawn), accompanied by a quick getaway. In that same moment, she hisses, while her hair spikes up in a horribly nasty way. Dad and Mom have always been crazy about her.

Poogie was our feline indicator as to Mom's condition these last few days. Every time Mom's condition or breathing status changed, Poogie's behavior would become erratic. We watched as she reacted… intuitively, catlike, and weirdly psychic. It got to the point where, in addition to monitoring my mother's status…we were watching the cat's behavior for any sign that Mom's condition had changed. She let us know when Mom had taken a turn for the worse, moving deeper into her coma, or when she had a fever. Poogie seemed to understand all that was going on with her owners, Bob and Georgie Forney.

Whenever Mom had a fever, Scott would sit beside her with a cool washcloth on her forehead until her temperature went down.

I would reach under her blanket, feeling her skin, adjusting the layers of bedding and rubbing her with lotion.

George handled his obvious pain differently, withdrawing at times to gather himself together.

Dad would bring her mouth moisture with water, using an eye dropper.

As time went on, each of our eyes revealed tattered, exposed sorrow.

Scott, Elizabeth, George and Dave left at night and returned in the morning, giving Dad and me some unwinding time. After my first night at their house I moved into their bedroom. I had opened my little cot on Mom's side of the bed, using the blanket I had been crocheting to cover up while Dad slept on the other side in their bed. Throughout the nights, we both reached out to touch her making sure she was still with us. We didn't sleep much since we were attuned to her every breath.

Palm Sunday came and Mom had moved into a deeper state of her coma. Her body hadn't changed its position, except as we needed to move it to care for her. Deborah had taught us how to lift her and to place a towel under her side, moving her body slightly so as to prevent bed sores. Since Mom had always slept in this position, we kept her in it because it was comfortable and familiar. On this morning, I asked Dad if I could open some blinds in the house and bring some Christian music into their room, which I did. Because of Moms sensitivity to light, we kept their bedroom blinds down.

Martha came by and sat for the last time with her friend, Georgie. I kept telling Mom it was "Hosanna Day." I reminded her that it was all ok, and that we were "right behind you," assuring her that soon we'd all be together, in dance and praises in Gods eternal place. That evening, I got on my knees beside her and sang, "Amazing Grace."

And then it began… the beginning of an abnormal pattern of breathing called Cheyne-Stokes.

As one would calculate birth labor contractions, often too, is the case of monitoring the breathing of a person dying. Like contractions, the breathing of a dying person can be counted and timed in anticipation of the end. Cheyne-Stokes is especially seen in people who have fallen into a coma. A persons breathing becomes shallow and deep. They will take several breaths… and then temporarily stop. The moments of 'stop' grow in length as end of life draws near. They may begin with a 10-15 second 'stop' and continue to slowly increase…eventually as long as 45-60 seconds in duration.

Mom began this breathing pattern late on Palm Sunday, and it lasted up until the final phase, which is called "the death rattle." This occurs as a result of saliva accumulation in the throat, causing a deep gurgle sound. The "death rattle" began minutes before we lost Mom.

Beside our parents' bed was a Mickey Mouse clock. We had begun to obsessively watch it once the Cheyne-Stokes had begun, silently counting. Scott, Dave or I would periodically mouth the seconds to each other. Our vigil had changed, and the three of us had suddenly become Mom's "Three Musketeers," counting, pacing and looking one another in the eye. We didn't talk to Dad about it but as soon as it began, the three of us were transported into a heightened state of anxiety and inevitably, a bonding experience of shared concern.

George, Scott and Elizabeth left late in the evening while Dave decided to stay with me, Dad and Mom.

Eventually, Dave made himself comfortable on the couch while Dad went to bed. I left a low light on in my parents' bedroom and pulled a chair up beside Mom. I sat in the chair, nodding in and out of sleep. Dad spoke to me, "Barb you need to go to bed." I ignored him, and continued to keep track of Mom's breathing. By midnight, she was having the Cheyne-Stokes apnea, with anywhere between 20-25 second breaks. Dad, once again, spoke to me. "Barb you need to go to bed. I don't feel it will be tonight." Once again, I ignored him. Finally, Dad got up and brought Dave a blanket and then he opened my cot. I was on one side of Mom while Dad was on the other. We both held her hand all night long. On Monday morning, Mom's apnea was close to the same pace. As the day wore on, her apnea increased to 25-35 seconds in silent intervals.

Britney, the hospice nurse that day, came around 11 am on Monday, March 25[th,] to check Mom's vitals. After our discussion on when she thought we might lose Mom, I made sure she had my personal directives in order. I had made it clear to hospice that, although we had chosen to care for Mom on our own when she died, I wanted a nurse to come over as soon as possible to help me attend to Mom before she left us for the crematorium.

George, Scott and Elizabeth came back that day. As evening came, George left while Dad got ready for bed. Dad intuitively knew it was going to be "tonight," and he wanted to be beside his wife as long as the last minutes before them would allow.

We gave them time together, listening to any changes coming from their bedroom. I quietly stepped into their room on and off, checking on Mom's breathing and giving her medicine as needed.

We knew it would to be soon. The intensity of love, alert and overflowing with emotion, was palpable. There is a fine line in honoring and respecting two people as they say their silent goodbyes. Dad had always said he wanted me with them when we lost Mom, yet I wanted to uphold the concept of, "when a man and a woman become husband and wife…" I wanted to be with Mom but I wanted God's will more. I wanted every moment that they had left together to be peaceful and I did not want to disturb or upset Dad as he said goodbye. Nonetheless, Mom still needed attending to, and all of us began to anxiously tip toe in and out of their room. Eventually Scott, Dave, and I were seated beside their bed. There was a low light on and the steady clock rhythm of "tick-tock-tick-tock" was the only sound in their house, along with Dads soft snore and Moms breathing.

When the time came for Mom to pass on from this world, Poogie stationed herself by my parent's bedroom door. She stood with her back to the rest of us and hissed that awful hiss, warning about what was to come. The death of our mom…

Who can wash away my sins, nothing but the blood of Jesus?

Side Note: It was very important to me to attend to Mom after she had died. In some ways it was like taking her off the cross, not literally of course, but to take her in my arms and prepare her body. Like in the days of Jesus. I knew my Mom would not be comfortable with a stranger handling her and I knew that if it were me, she would have done the same.

Betty, the hospice nurse on duty that night, came to help me. I was very happy to see Betty since she had helped us when Mom was at her worst one day. Although she couldn't communicate it at the time, Mom visibly liked her. Together, Betty and I took care of Mom. Life is sometimes odd. One of the most sacred hours of my life was spent with this loving, thoughtful and compassionate woman. She was our chosen hospice nurse for "such a time as this." I knew nothing else about her… yet, she is now etched in my heart.

Dad called George with the news that Mom had passed on and he immediately returned to say his goodbye.

When the coroner came to remove Mom from the house, I took Dave out into the driveway to be alone with him as we waved Mom off. Betty came alongside Dad at the bottom of the outside stairs so that he was in good hands and not alone. I knew that this would be my deepest moment of anguish, as my dear mother was being taken away from us for what felt like forever. I knew my husband was the only one I was able to lean on for my last goodbye. My legs gave way beneath me as Dave held me up, reminding me that this was not the end.

Brothers and sisters, we do not want you to be uninformed about those who sleep in death, so that you do not grieve like the rest of mankind, who have no hope. For we believe that Jesus died and rose again, and so we believe that God will bring with Jesus those who have fallen asleep in him. According to the Lord's word, we tell you that we who are still alive, who are left until the coming of the Lord, will certainly not precede those who have fallen asleep. For the

Lord himself will come down from heaven, with a loud command, with the voice of the archangel and with the trumpet call of God, and the dead in Christ will rise first. After that, we who are still alive and are left will be caught up together with them in the clouds to meet the Lord in the air. And so we will be with the Lord forever. Therefore encourage one another with these words.

Thessalonians 4:13-18

What's up Doc?

Just the Facts: "As a family caregiver, you are grieving throughout the entire process, not only with the death of your loved one," says Suzanne Mintz, president and co-founder of the National Family Caregivers Association, who cares for her MS-afflicted husband and whose father also died from Alzheimer's five years ago. "You grieve with each loss -- each time they go down a notch, with each reminder of what was and what it has become."

"Mom bought me a gift for my college graduation. It was a Newton's Cradle Multi-Ball Pendulum for the Office. You know, it is a classic desk toy also known as 'Balance Balls,' 'Newton's Pendulum,' 'Kinetic Balls' and 'Newton's Balls.' This executive office toy demonstrates the law of conservation of momentum—I had to say that as my son, Zachary is studying physics, so he needs to know Mom got me a gadget that demonstrated the law of conservation of momentum! These balls hang from a metal cradle using fishing line and you swing one ball to hit another ball, that hits the next, and so on. The inscription on the gift says, 'In the Front Row' which was a special message that Mom shared with me often. I think she was proud of me and wanted me to always know that as far as she was concerned, I was in the front row. Whenever I would have a tough day at work, I would think about those balls and remember the smile on Mom's face when she would say, 'You are in the front row."

Spoken by Georgie and Bob's son, Scott- Our Family Representative at Mom's Memorial Service.

"Georgie always shared her welcoming smile with a 'Hey you!' You just knew she was happy to see you and that nothing else mattered at the moment. I could always depend on her to be at school, setting up her classroom way before the start date, being there late hours during the school year, and also there after the kids were gone in June. If I wanted to take a break or see another face, she was there. Georgie was always willing to give an attentive ear and was intuitive of knowing when it was needed. She rejoiced in our accomplishments and was there during difficult times, always willing to help."

Spoken by Georgie's friend, Gayle-a fellow teacher of Mom's who shared at Mom's Memorial Service.

"Georgie was a very special compassionate and supportive friend. I admired her intellect, her understanding of her kindergarteners needs, her rapport with anyone that came into her life, and most of all, her love for her Savior."

Spoken by Georgie and Bob's friend Martha-The Keeper of the Books at Mom's Memorial Service.

"Georgie Forney passed away on March 26, 2013."

"You know, it's funny, but saying that one sentence sounds so impersonal...almost matter of fact, but it also happens to be true."
"It's been just over three weeks since Georgie left us, but saying that one sentence doesn't seem to do justice to, or tell the story of her illness. It doesn't capture the roller coaster of emotions which were so prevalent during the months, weeks, or days leading toward her decline."

"*That one sentence* doesn't come close to addressing how the worlds of each family member were turned upside down with her loss, or the utter sense of grief and heartbreak that accompanied it when she drew her last breath."

"*That one sentence* says nothing that comes close to addressing the humble caring kindness which was shown by the visiting nurses from Androscoggin Hospice...And the sincere, heartfelt appreciation that those special ladies so warmly deserve."

"*That one sentence* doesn't speak to the love and patience of Georgie's husband, Bob, who through tears, sleepless nights, and a fractured heart would tirelessly immerse and devote himself so completely to Georgie's love and care…that, in doing so, would gladly jeopardize his own health and wellbeing.

It's one thing to talk about love…it's quite another to witness it in action. And when you do, as my wife and I did…It is both a privilege and a blessing."

"Georgie Forney passed away on March 26, 2013…"

Spoken by Georgie and Bob's son-in-law, Dave-The lay Pastor at Mom's Memorial Service.

Shortly before we lost Mom, Dad and I discussed a future Memorial Service for her. Mom and Dad have directives in order that they don't want a funeral but Mom specified that her children could do something if they chose, along the line of a memorial. After talking the service possibilities over with Dad, I consulted with my brothers about what we might do. We decided that to have a memorial service at Stevens Book Elementary School Library, where she had taught, would be a lovely way to honor Mom. Martha offered to secure the use of the library since she thought it was a wonderful idea. We are grateful that the school was so accommodating with our request and a date was set soon after we lost Mom.

On April 17th, 22 days after Mom went to be with God, we had a beautiful service for her. Kim came and played the piano, Martha and Gayle spoke and honored their friend and colleague. Scott represented the family and he talked about our Mom. Our children, Yana, Tracy, and Nate, each did a reading. Dave officiated the service. Aunt Donna Rae's children, Debbie and Jerry, came to pay their respects.

The library, which Mom had such an endearment to, was where she was memorialized. It is a room with a stain glassed alcove in which a rocking chair sits. It is a room full of sunlight and children's books. It is a room tended to by her very good friend and fellow Christian sister, Martha. It is a room Mom would have taken each of us by the hand and walked through, telling us stories about the books, the kids and Stevens Brook's staff. We could see her face, her smile and feel her lingering love for us on that day…

In the spring, the school gave my brother Scott permission to build a small reading room within the library for "wittle people" to sit in with their books. Martha made suggestions and helped to get Mr. Liddy, a local carpenter, to fabricate it. Hence, on any given school day in Bridgeton, Maine, at the Stevens Brook Elementary School Library, one can walk through the door and see a nugget of a house with a copper roof and sign saying, "Georgie's Reading Place".

Mom's brother, Gerald Walizer, had been a teacher himself. He taught high school history and was a rare and remarkable man. Uncle Jerry died when he was 46 years old, from cancer. He too, was a piano player and Mom idolized him. She also had a deep affection for her father, George Kenneth Walizer. Her Dad had a nickname for everyone, and Mom's was "Doc." These two men treated Mom with delightful teasing charm. She was the baby of the family and they never let her forget it. She had their peculiar sense of humor and an adventurous spirit. Mom loved that she had gone to a one room schoolhouse as a youngster. She loved Water Street, the Dyke, the Susquehanna River, the hills, and her Pennsylvania heritage. Though she had left it many years ago, she never ever turned her back on it.

I think that Mom secretly prized being a kindergarten teacher more than just about anything else. I think that, in her heart of hearts, she was a kindred spirit to her brother Jerry, and she knew it. I think she wished more than just about anything else on her wish list, that he had been here when she became a teacher. I think she knew he would have been so thrilled for his baby sister.

Mom was a teacher. The word itself made her giggle aloud. "I'm a teacher," she'd say. For Mom, being a teacher was like a "pinch me moment" over and over again. Mom emptied herself out as a teacher. It was her life's purpose and ministry. It was not just a job, it was a joy and a privilege to her.

After getting her Bachelor Degree, she enrolled in Antioch College to acquire her Master's Degree. Around the time that Mom retired, she talked about going on for her Doctorate. She went as far as researching schools. Her illness got in the way, and almost as soon as she was considering going back to school, those thoughts drifted away. It makes me smile to think about how proud of his "Doc" my grandfather would have been.

Mom wasn't just a teacher, she was an extraordinary human being. She had the kind of character I envy; goodness, merciful, gentle, slow to anger, eager to help, patient, forgiving, long suffering, thoughtful and sincerely loving. I am not some delusional daughter, falsely glorifying a mother because she is gone. Mom really was that kind of a lady, and she made it seem so easy. She was the kind of woman who lived for the day when God would say to her…

"Well done, good and faithful servant! You have been faithful with a few things; I will put you in charge of many things. Come and share your Master's happiness."
Matthew 25:23

Side Note: As we sojourn through grief, bracing ourselves for the expected "first birthday" or "Mother's Day," it is more than that. Grief occurs in those unexpected minutes. It is the walk to the attic to pull out a box of Christmas decorations and seeing all those collected treasures given to us by our mothers. It is in reaching out to pick up the box when our body gives way to an uncontrollable shock and reality. It's when our inner most being wells up in such sadness and pain we wish we could run, yet we are frozen. Grief and mourning hit us like a flood and there is no protection or relief. It is the throbbing in our head and temple that you wish you could push off with hands which are busily working to wipe away seemingly never ending tears. It is found on a couch, cradling our bodies reverted into a baby position and draped in a blanket. It is in the moment when silence hears her voice and you remember she is gone, as you feel her skin and hand crossing your bare arm. It is on the face no longer there, smiling, just inches from your own. It is the anticipation of laughter walking through the door, or the advice no longer on the other end of the phone. It is the quiet in the middle of the night, when it dawns on your whole being that she isn't here. You are not going to see her in the morning. It is a knot in your throat and a trembling in your stomach that grows into an earthquake in mere seconds, and pours out in internal screams and frantic sobbing.

It hurts…really hurts.

Writing this book has been helpful in processing the events in my parent's lives throughout their walk with Alzheimer's. It has helped me to put some things to rest, and it has illuminated some memories which will take time to let go of.

I found that it is difficult to deal with grief publicly. As progressed as we humans claim to be, we can sometimes be really insensitive. I have found that it is important to say to a person, dealing with loss, "Tell me all about it…" and mean it. It is valuable to the ones left behind, to be able to speak about their sadness; in detail if need be. For those of us grieving, it is an ongoing journey.

I have jokingly said to my husband that before losing Mom I really didn't "get it." I wasn't able to understand what a person felt, because I didn't have the experience. Now, I say that I am in the "I got it" club. For some time after losing Mom, I felt badly about my lack of empathy in the past. I wanted to return and find those people, along the way who had suffered, and say, "I am so sorry" and "How are you, really?"

In my own bereavement, I found out quickly that, many who shared in this form of heartache were hastily transported into their own memories. I often left a conversation disconcerted by my own need to "talk," while instead, listening to stories upon stories of loss. It was in this venue of writing that my own "time heals" began to happen.

Alzheimer's is a crazy illness. Caring for a person who has this debilitating, progressive aliment can leave an individual with traumatic residue. We are left with memories of a person who is "not themselves." We bear firsthand witness of their minds leaving them and their bodies unable to properly respond. There is quilt at even having had the thought that they would be better off and at peace, "if God would just take them home." It is a long, painful goodbye.

Knowing what is to come, does not soften the reality when it does come. Thinking we are prepared for death isn't the same as facing it. "Goodbye" in death means gone. It means, "I won't see you anymore." That is the stark, raw sting of grief. Wrapping our minds around this takes time, and trusting in God for the future takes faith. It is the intangible longing of hope.

My hope is that this memoir reveals the character of the woman who bore me 55 years ago. My hope is that I have honored God in truth and declaration of His steadfast faithfulness. My hope is that, along the way, this book may be helpful for someone caring for and attending to a loved one with Alzheimer's or dementia.

Books were so special to her. Not ebooks, mind you, but books whose pages you could hold, touch and feel.

I miss my mother, and I cannot wait to one day embrace her in my arms again, talk and laugh with her.

Marantha !

Just the Facts

Bibliography of web sites

Chapter 1
http://www.alz.org/alzheimers_disease_facts_and_figures.asp

Chapter 2
http://www.webmd.com/alzheimers/alzheimers-disease-stages

Chapter 3
http://www.alzinfo.org/04/articles/caregiving-26

Chapter 4
http://www.webmd.com/alzheimers/alzheimers-disease-stages?page=2

Chapter 5
http://aphasia.org.au/public/resources/public-aphasia-cards/

Chapter 6
http://www.alz.org/care/alzheimers-mid-moderate-stage-caregiving.asp

Chapter 7
http://www.cdc.gov/Features/Alzheimers/

Chapter 8
http://www.livestrong.com/article/109380-last-stages-alzheimers-disease/

Chapter 9
http://www.alzheimer.ca/en/About-dementia/Alzheimer-s-disease/Stages-of-
Alzheimer-s-   disease/End-of-Life

Chapter 10
http://www.hospicefoundation.org/deathsigns

Chapter 11
http://www.webmd.com/alzheimers/features/caregiver-grief-triggers-mixed-
emotions

All scripture taken from Oxford NIV Scofield Study Bible 1984

"Even to your old age and gray hairs

I am he, I am he who will sustain you.

I have made you and I will carry you; I will sustain you and I will rescue you."

Isaiah 46:4